the Brownie

ANNUAL 1988

edited by Rosalind Woodhouse

Busy Betsy Brownie 42
Make your own mobile
Brownie

Brownies on Skids! 44
Bridgend Brownies visit a
Police Museum and a skid
pan

Stitches to Send 46
Why not *sew* a card instead
of *writing* one?

**The Private Life of
the Robin** 48
All about Britain's favourite
bird

Ratty and Mole's Picnic 50
Read about their river outing
and the food they took with
them

Knit a Brownie Doll 55
For yourself or as a gift for
someone else

The Lego Story 56
Building bricks as you've
never seen them before

**How Does Your Garden
Grow?** 60
Collages from seed catalogues!

Puzzle Answers 62
Plus last year's competition
winners

Competition
Read about this year's
exciting competition

front cover photograph by
Christopher Phillips
back cover photograph by
Marion Wale

Copyright © MCMLXXXVII by The Girl Guides Association
All rights reserved throughout the world
Published in Great Britain by
World International Publishing Limited
An Egmont Company
Egmont House, P.O. Box 111, Great Ducie Street
Manchester M60 3BL
Printed in Great Britain

ISBN 7235 6800 6

Come Fly a Kite

written and photographed by Susan Tyte

illustrated by Linda Sandey

Have you ever been fascinated by a colourful kite flying through the air? Or had fun making a kite swoop and dance as you held the string? If you want to learn about kites, and how to make them just read on...

Lift Off!

The name 'kite' comes from the large bird of prey which uses its wings to hover. Both sorts of kite stay airborne because their weight is supported by the wind pushing from below. A kite can be made from any light material structured over a frame, and with a cord or line to anchor it to the ground. A tail helps it to balance in flight, and it certainly adds to a kite's effect, as it streams behind, drawing patterns in the air.

Kite Tales

The first kites were made 2500 years ago in China. They were probably made of ricepaper or silk stretched over a light-weight bamboo frame.

Kite flying was introduced to Europe in the 16th century by merchant traders who brought back kites from the Orient as toys for their children.

In modern Japan, when a baby boy is born, a kite is flown outside the family's house to take thanks up to the gods.

Every 5th May, the Japanese hold a festival where fish-shaped kites are flown. It is believed that they bring courage and strength to the person holding the string. Some kites are so large that twelve or more people are needed to hold them down!

Japanese kites can fight! Fliers make the cord of their kite cross that of an opponent. By jerking down on the line, the string is cut and the kite is kept by the victor.

Flights of Fancy

'Climbing the Heights' is a Chinese festival, celebrating a legend. A man dreamed of a great misfortune happening to his family on a certain day. When that day arrived, he took all his family out to the highest hill to fly kites. On returning home, he found that his house had burned to the ground. He was so grateful that his family was safe that he vowed each year to give thanks to the gods by going out to fly kites.

Musical kites are made in the East by attaching miniature gongs and reed pipes to the strings. The wind blows the instruments into life, wailing and chiming.

Ancient Chinese armies flew 'musical' kites over enemy armies, to pretend that they were surrounded by evil spirits. The terrified invaders ran away!

General Han Hsin was besieging a fortress, and to find out the distance between his army and the fort, he flew a kite over the walls. By measuring the kite string he knew how far to tunnel in order to get behind the wall and surprise his enemies.

Kites in Use

A Japanese architect used kites to lift work materials to his men at the top of buildings.

Indonesian fishermen make kites from leaves. These are flown from boats. Attached to the kite tail is a hook which trails in the water. Fish take the bait and the fisherman gets his catch.

A famous experiment was carried out by Benjamin Franklin, later President of America, who wanted to prove that electricity was made during a thunderstorm. He tied a key to his kite string, and flew the kite during a storm. When the kite was brought down the key was found to be charged with electricity.

Weathermen make many observations using cameras and thermometers attached to kite strings.

Bright yellow kites were given to wartime pilots, to be flown if they were shot down, in order to guide search planes to the area.

A bridge over the River Niagara was built with the help of a kite which carried construction cables to the opposite bank.

The early aeroplanes, such as the Wright Brothers' Kittyhawk, were little more than box kites with an engine.

Kite Records

Charles Lindburgh, the first man to fly the Atlantic, set the world record when, in 1919, he flew eight kites strung together to a height of 9,758 metres.

Baden Baden-Powell, brother of the Chief Scout, constructed the first kite capable of lifting a man.

For Safety's Sake

Do not fly a kite in the rain or during a thunderstorm.
Do not use wire as a line.
Do not fly a kite near trees or powerlines.
Do not fly a kite near an aerodrome.
Do not fly a kite so high that it interferes with aircraft.

Now where's a good place to begin?

And time for a rest at the end of a good meeting.

Plenty of space here . . .

Let's Make a Kite

written by Susan Tyte

illustrated by Linda Sandey

One evening in June, Brownies of the 27th Kingswood (Christchurch) Downend Pack spent their meeting kite-making. It took about half an hour for each Brownie to make her kite and that left plenty of time to try them out.

If you want to make a kite like theirs, this is what you do:

You Need

An oblong of light-weight fabric, plastic or tissue paper (an old carrier bag will do), measuring 60cm by 40cm.

A piece of paper 10cm by 5cm.

Two strips of strong card ½cm wide and 60cm long.

A paper clip.

Twenty metres of string.

A lolly stick.

A stick of glue.

A ruler, pencil and scissors.

Sellotape

What You Do

Working on a covered surface, take the material and measure a line across the width, 20cm from the top.

Now draw a line lengthways down the centre. Join the ends of the four lines.

Cut out the 'diamond' shape for your kite and keep the scraps for its tail. Now follow the photographs:

1. Glue the strips of card down the width and length of the kite. (You will have to trim them to the right length.)

6

2. Turn the kite over.

3. Take the piece of paper and fold it lengthways. Open it up and make two cuts as far as the centre fold, in one half. Fold the centre tab backwards.

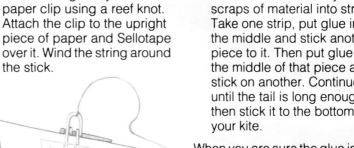

4. Now stick it to the centre of the kite so that half the paper stands up.

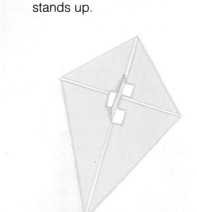

5. Tie the string firmly to the paper clip using a reef knot. Attach the clip to the upright piece of paper and Sellotape over it. Wind the string around the stick.

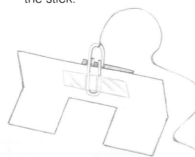

6. Now make a tail! Cut your scraps of material into strips. Take one strip, put glue in the middle and stick another piece to it. Then put glue in the middle of that piece and stick on another. Continue until the tail is long enough, then stick it to the bottom of your kite.

When you are sure the glue is dry and you have read the safety points – go fly your kite!

Have fun!

THE WRESTLING PRINCESS

Once upon a time there was a princess who was six feet tall, who liked her own way and who loved to wrestle. Every day, she would challenge the guards at her father's palace to wrestling matches and every day, she won. Then she would pick up the loser and fling him on the ground, but gently, because she had a very kind nature.

The princess had one other unusual hobby. She liked to drive fork-lift trucks. Because she was a princess, and her father was very rich, she had three fork-lift trucks of her own — a blue one, a yellow one, and a green and purple striped one, with a coronet on each side.

One day, when the princess had wrestled with sixteen soldiers at once and had beaten them all, the king sent a page to tell her to come to see him in the royal tea-room.

The princess was annoyed. "Is it urgent?" she asked the page. "I was just greasing the axle of my blue fork-lift truck."

"I think you should come, Your Highness," said the page, respectfully. "His Majesty was in a terrible temper. He's burnt four pieces of toast already and dripped butter all over his second-best ermine robe."

"Oh gosh," said the princess, "I'd better come right away."

She got up, picked up her oilcan and went into the royal bathroom to wash her hands for tea. She left oil marks all over the gold taps and the page sent a message to the palace house-keeper to clean them quickly before the king saw them.

The princess went down to the tea-room and knocked loudly on the door. A herald opened it. "The Princess Ermyntrude!" he announced loudly.

"About time too," said the king. "And where have you been?"

"Greasing the axle of the blue fork-lift truck," answered the princess politely.

The king put his head in his hands and groaned.

"This can't go on," he sighed tragically. "When *will* you stop messing about with these dirty machines, Ermyntrude? You're nearly sixteen and you need a husband. I must have a successor."

"I'll succeed you, Father," cried the princess cheerfully. "I'd love to be a king."

"You can't be a king," said the king sadly. "It's not allowed."

"Why not?" asked the princess.

"I don't know," said the king. "I don't make the laws. Ask the judges — it's their affair. Anyway, you can't and that's that. You have to have a husband, and you won't get a husband if you don't change your ways."

"Why ever not?" asked the princess, in surprise.

"To get a husband you must be enchantingly beautiful, dainty and weak," said the king.

"Well, I'm not," said Ermyntrude cheerfully. "I'm nothing to look at, I'm six feet tall and I'm certainly not weak."

"Ermyntrude!" said the king. "If you want a husband, you will have to become delicate and frail."

"I don't *want* a husband," said the princess. "*You* want me to have a husband. I just want to go on wrestling and looking after my trucks."

"Well, you can't," said the king. "And that's that. I shall lock up the fork-lift trucks, instruct the guards that there is to be no more wrestling, and we shall have a contest to find you a husband."

The princess was furiously angry. "Just you wait," she shouted rudely. "I'll ruin your stupid old contest. How dare you lock up my fork-lift trucks."

"Ermyntrude," said the king sternly, "you will do as you are told."

The first contest to find a prince to marry Princess Ermyntrude

8

took place the next day. The king had beamed a message by satellite to all the neighbouring countries, and helicopters with eligible princes in them were arriving by the dozen at the palace heliport.

The princess watched them from the window of her room, where she was sulking. "Stupid, stupid, stupid," she said. "Why, not one of them even pilots his own helicopter." And she went on sulking.

After lunch, the king sent a messenger to announce that the princess was to dress in her best robes and come to the great hall of the palace.

She put on her golden dress, her fur cape, her small golden crown and her large golden shoes (for she had big feet), and down she went.

Seated inside were seventy-two princes, all seeking her hand in marriage. The princess looked at them. They all looked back.

"Good afternoon and welcome," began the king. "We are here today to find a suitable husband for the lovely Princess

Ermyntrude with one of her trucks.

Ermyntrude, my daughter. The first competition in this contest will be that of height. The princess cannot have a husband shorter than herself, so you will all line up while the Lord Chamberlain measures you."

The seventy-two princes lined up in six rows and the Lord Chamberlain took out the royal tape measure and began to measure them.

"Forty-eight princes left in the contest, Your Majesty," cried the Lord Chamberlain.

"The second competition," said the king, "will be that of disposition. Princess Ermyntrude has a beautiful disposition, none better, but she does have a slightly hasty temper. She cannot have a husband who cannot match her temper. So we shall have a face-pulling, insult-throwing contest. The Lord Chamberlain will call your names one by one and you will come forward to confront the princess, pull the worst face you can manage, put on a temper display and insult her."

The first prince stepped forward. Princess Ermyntrude pulled a repulsive face and he burst into tears.

"Eliminated," said the Lord Chamberlain, running forward with a box of tissues. "Next!" The next and the next after him *and* the prince following them, were all eliminated and it was not until the fifth competitor crossed his eyes, stuck out his tongue and shouted, "Silly cry baby," at the princess, making her so angry that she forgot to shout back, that anyone succeeded at all.

The fifth prince inspired the next four, but the princes after that were no match for Princess Ermyntrude, until the eighteenth and nineteenth princes called her, "Crow face" and "Squiggle bum" and made her giggle.

By the end of the contest, there were only seven princes left, all taller and more insulting than the princess.

"And now," said the king, "for the third and final contest. As you may know, Princess Ermyntrude

is very strong. She cannot have a weaker husband, so you will all line up and wrestle with her."

The Lord Chamberlain lined up the seven princes. Just as they were being given their instructions, the princess, who was flexing her arm muscles, glanced over at the watching crowd of commoners and noticed a short man covered in helicopter engine oil standing at the back. As she looked, he looked back at her and winked quite distinctly. The princess looked again. The short man winked again.

"*Helicopter* engine oil!" thought the princess. "That's the sort of man I like."

Just then the short man looked at her and, forming his mouth carefully, whispered, "Choose the seventh. Don't beat him."

Princess Ermyntrude didn't much like the look of the seventh prince but she did want to please the helicopter mechanic so she nodded discreetly, rolled up her golden sleeves and stepped forward to take on the first prince. CRASH! He hit the mat with staggering force. CRASH, CRASH, CRASH, CRASH, CRASH.

The next five princes followed. The poor seventh prince was looking paler and paler and his knees were beginning to buckle under him. The princess looked quickly at the mechanic, who nodded briefly, then she moved towards the seventh prince. He seized her feebly by the arm.

"Good heavens, I could floor him with one blow," thought the princess, but she didn't. Instead, she let herself go limp and floppy and two seconds later, for the first time in her life, she lay flat on her back on the floor.

The poor prince looked very pale.

"This is terrible, terrible," he muttered desperately.

"Nonsense," cried the king. "I award you the hand of the princess and half my kingdom."

"But Sire . . ." stammered the prince, "I can't."

"Can't!" shouted the king. "What do you mean can't. You

continued on page 58 9

A DAY IN THE LIFE OF A VET

photographs by Christopher Phillips

If you have a pet at home, perhaps you have visited a vet's surgery at some time.

Animals can be injured, or become sick, just as we can, but unlike us, they do not visit the doctor; they are taken to see a *veterinary surgeon* (a 'vet').

I went to see Mr Trevor Turner in Northolt, Middlesex, where he runs the Mandeville Veterinary Hospital. He explained to me all about his job and the animals he sees every day.

Mr Turner's working day begins with an early morning check on animals in the wards. These are not like hospital wards, with rows of beds, but rooms of big, comfortable cages with blankets for the pets to sleep on. Every pet has a cage of its own, and beside each door there is a card giving the animal's name, and the reason it needs treatment.

At about 9am, Mr Turner holds the first 'clinic' of the day, when people bring in their pets to be examined. After a short wait in the reception area, with their owners, they are brought into one of the consulting rooms.

Often, an animal may be nervous of being handled by a stranger, but vets are trained to treat pets gently, but firmly, so that they don't become too frightened.

Mr Turner may decide that an animal needs to be given medicine, or a blood test. These, and many other jobs are done by *veterinary nurses*.

Frisky, this tan and white bitch needs a small operation before she is accepted as a 'Hearing Dog for the Deaf'. She is clearly very fond of her nurse!

Here, a nurse is about to put a blood sample into a machine called a centrifuge. This separates out the different ingredients of the blood, and helps the vet to learn more about what is wrong with that particular animal.

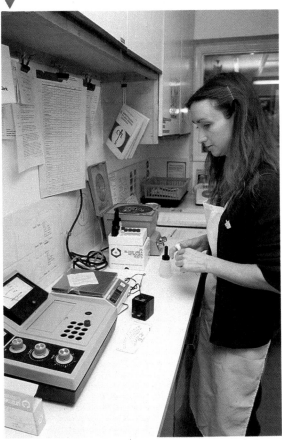

Nurses also help with operations. Mr Turner starts operating at about 10am; the number of operations varies from day to day. Often they are needed to treat animals hurt in road traffic accidents ('R.T.A.s' to the surgery staff).

The equipment in the operating theatre is very modern and similar to that used in our hospitals. Operations are carried out under general anaesthetic, which makes the animals unconscious, and therefore unable to feel any pain. Big metal canisters in a store room near the surgery contain the anaesthetic gases.

Animals with fractures (broken bones) have them reset under anaesthetic. To keep the re-set bones in the right position, Mr Turner applies plaster bandages. In this picture, he is changing 'Spike's' plaster (Spike's ankle and hip were hurt in a R.T.A.).

It is very important to keep the surroundings and all of the instruments very clean, so the entire operating theatre and its contents are cleaned every day.

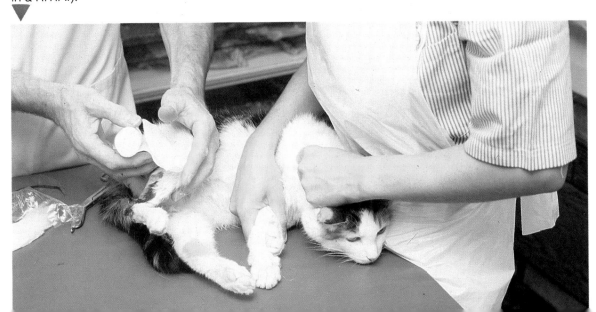

▲

Not all of the animals cared for at the Mandeville Hospital need operations. In the afternoon at around 4pm, Mr Turner has another consulting session; some of the animals he sees may just need medicine, like Sooty the poodle, seen here being weighed. Others may need to be kept in for treatment, or observation, to find out what is wrong with them.

The bulldog in this picture is being fed by means of a drip feed, while his condition is assessed; the nurse is adjusting the sticking plaster which attached the tube to his leg.

Not all of the animals at the Mandeville Veterinary Hospital are there because they are ill. Mr and Mrs Turner are very fond of all kinds of animals, they have lots of pets (four cats, four dogs, a rat, guinea pig, rabbit, two chinchillas and two tortoises, at the last count!).

▼

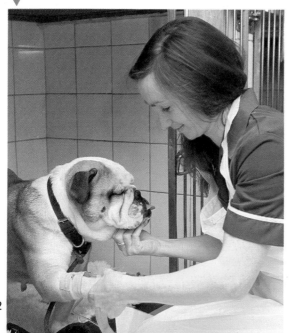

Some of them, like Panda a six year old buck rabbit were left at the Hospital because their owners couldn't look after them any longer. ▼

When I left the Hospital, Mr Turner's day was far from over. After another consulting session at 6.30pm, he would then be on call late into the evening, in case any animals needed emergency treatment. Just in time for an early night, and a 6.30am start the next day.

The Brownie Annual would like to thank Mr and Mrs Trevor Turner, and all the staff of the Mandeville Veterinary Hospital for their help in producing this feature.

ROPE BRACELET

by Jil Shipley

Make this great rope bracelet in just a few minutes. Make it with luminous, brightly coloured rope from a sailing shop or with silky cord, thick string or even sisal rope. You need 50cm. of rope for each bracelet, any thickness is fine. Make lots! Just follow the step by step diagrams. It looks complicated but once you start, it's actually terribly easy!

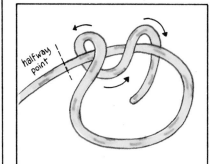

Start the knot at the halfway point - loop one end around as shown.

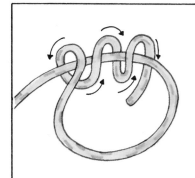

Make three loops (or four or five if you prefer).

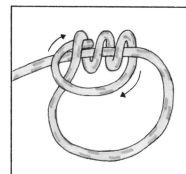

Bring the short end round and into the loops.

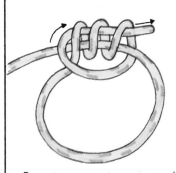

Pull the short end right through the loops.

Tighten the knot and cut off the loose end.

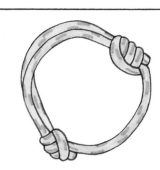

Make a similar knot with the other end. Adjust the size by pulling the second knot.

SPECS and SPEEDY

BY Viv Quillin

The Brownies are camping in Lady Acre's grounds. Brown Owl prepares them for tomorrow's hike.

...very important not to forget...

One-something to eat two-something to drink three-take a map ...and we set off at nine o'clock.

Next morning

Brown Owl said half past nine ...didn't she?

Here's a sign! They've gone without us— we'd better catch up!

But first let's check the list of things to bring. One-something to read... in case we get bored I suppose.

I'm reading my first aid book. I'm taking the test next week.

Number two-some invisible ink, I can't think why Brown Owl wants us to bring that!

Number three —make a hat.

I've made one too!

RIDDLE-ME-REE

Find the letter in each line to make three words.

My first is in brown but not in red
My second is in tree but not in leaf
My third is in good but not in bad
My fourth is in Pow-wow but not in ring
My fifth is in journey but not in pathway
My sixth is in Six but not in Pack
My seventh is NOT in you but is in me
My eighth is in games but not in work

My first is in Pack but not in Six
My second is in Promise but not in Law
My third is in Ranger and also in Guide

My first is in fix but not in mend
My second is in four but not in five
My third is in one and also in none

When you have found all three,
I hope you'll agree!

BROWNIE CROSSWORD

by Helen Lane

Fit the following words into the grid below:

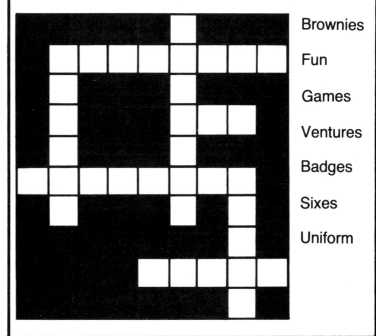

Brownies

Fun

Games

Ventures

Badges

Sixes

Uniform

PUZZLE SQUARES

by Ann Hillyer

In this puzzle square, the letters can be used to make lots of girls' names. Using each letter once only, including the large A in the centre, see how many you can find!

1 across   A knitting stitch

1 down   Fill a suitcase

2 down   Not win

3 across   A flying toy

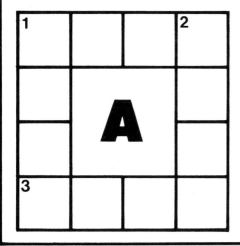

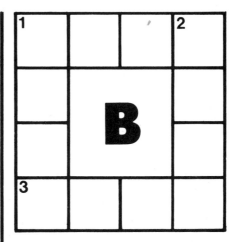

In this puzzle square there are at least twenty words beginning with S. You may use each letter once only, including the large B in the centre. See how many you can puzzle out in 5 minutes!

1 across   Winter dish

1 down   Farmer's bag

2 down   Compass point

3 across   Kind of skirt

Christmas Eggs

by Wendy Atkinson
illustrated by David Brian

For each decoration, you will need:

An egg
Nail scissors
Enamel or poster paint
nail varnish
gold or silver spray
Lace, sequins or glitter
Glue
Gold or silver thread
1 tablespoon washing powder
Small cake decoration

1. With the nail scissors cut an oval in the eggshell and carefully remove the egg. (Carefully 'jab' the scissors in, then make very small cuts and the shell will not break.) Wash out the shell.

2. Holding the egg shell with your fingers inside the hole, paint or varnish it and leave to dry.

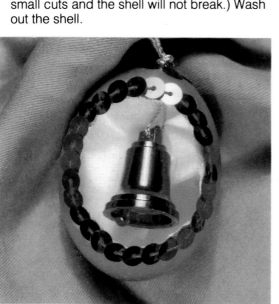

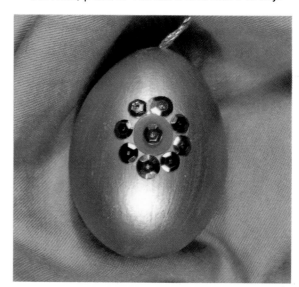

18

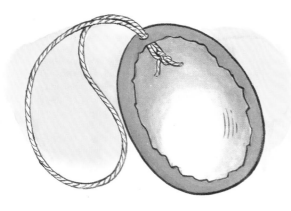

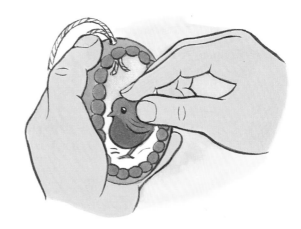

3. Make a hole in the top of the egg. This is where the egg is most likely to crack, so be very gentle. Use the point of the scissors and twist downwards and forwards until you pierce a hole – you need to be patient! Double a piece of thread and knot it firmly. Then, using a thin piece of wire, pass the thread through the hole.

5. Mix the washing powder with a *very little* water to make a paste, and place it in the bottom of the egg. Gently press the cake decoration in and leave to dry.

4. Glue the opening and use lace, glitter or sequins to decorate the edge. It is also a good idea to decorate the hole at the top to strengthen it. You can decorate the rest of the outside of the egg with sequins or beads. A single pattern of sequins on the back is very effective.

When it is completely dry, hang it on your Christmas tree.

These make unusual Christmas presents and by collecting oddments of lace, sequins and beads, or even little pasta shapes every one can be different.

George Pushdragon and his wonderful CATS

by Hilda Young

Victoria

Thomas Stearns Eliot was born at St Louis Missouri, on September 26, 1888. Even as a child he was always extremely fond of cats, and during his lifetime he owned a series of cats with such delightful names as Wiscus, Pettipaws and George Pushdragon. He even took over George's name whenever he wanted to conceal his own identity when he entered crossword competitions!

Perhaps it was this love of cats which gave him the idea of writing a series of rhymes about several strange and wonderful cats, for the amusement of the small children of his publishers and their friends. They loved these verses and asked for more, and Uncle Tom, who had a mischievous streak in his nature (he loved buying tricks from joke shops to play on his friends) was more than willing to oblige. When his book was finally published it was dedicated to several young friends and also the mysterious Man in White Spats.

Naming a Cat

Uncle Tom insisted that every cat should have *three* names. The first one plain, and used every-day, such as James, George or perhaps Thomas. Next, a rather peculiar or unusual name such as Plato, Munkustrap, Quaxo or Jellylorum, and finally, the secret name which is given to a cat by itself, known only unto the cat... a very special name indeed!

Kind and Criminal Cats

Each of Uncle Tom's cats has its own very special personality. There is Jennyanydots, who is a Gumbie Cat. All day long she sits on the mat, but at night she is very busy indeed making a mouse-cake of bread and dried peas, or a beautiful fry of lean bacon and cheese for her mice friends.

She also keeps the cockroaches out of mischief by drilling them and turning them out as a well-disciplined troop of helpful Boy Scouts with their own Beetles' Tattoo!

But Mungojerrie and Rumpleteazer are two notorious criminal cats who live in Victoria Square, well-known cat burglars, who are so confident that they even engage the policeman in conversation, before looking for a window left ajar to steal the joint from the oven!

But they cannot compare with the master criminal Macavity, the Mystery Cat, who's broken every law... even the law of gravity! His whiskers are uncombed and his coat very dusty, but he can steal anything from the milk to a Treaty from the War Office, and get away with it each time, because when the crime is discovered...Macavity's not there!

Growltiger and Lady Griddlestone

The Oldest Cat of All

The oldest cat of all is Old Deuteronomy, who had buried nine wives before Queen Victoria came to the throne! He believes his great age allows him to flout the law and he refuses to move out of the middle of the High Street even on market day! Because of the chaos this causes, a 'Road Closed' notice had to be put up!

Cats, at Work and Play

Some cats work very hard... others spend their lives in a round of pleasure and fun.

Growltiger is a barge cat, known as 'The Terror of the Thames', no goose or hen was safe from him, but he lost his fight with a Siamese cat and has a badly mauled ear as a result! He once had a mate aboard the barge called Grumbuskin, but now Growltiger has a love in his life... the Lady Griddlestone whom he serenades each night in his manly baritone voice while his crew sleep below in their barrel beds.

The theatre has its share of acting cats. Mr Mistoffelees, is a small, quiet, black cat but also a wonderful conjuror who can walk on the narrowest rail and play lots of tricks with a cork or a spoon... or a bit of fish-paste!

Gus, whose full name is Asparagus and who once acted with Sir Henry Irving, received *seven* cat calls from his admiring gallery audience when he played Firefrorefiddle, the Fiend of the Fells!

Another hard-working cat is Skimbleshanks, the Railway Cat, who signals the train's departure with his glass-green eyes and away he goes, making sure that the Night Mail Train is on time, and travels to Crewe and Carlisle... and even Dumfries while its passengers sleep!

In sharp contrast, Bustopher Jones is a fat cat–about–town who tours the smartest eating spots for winkles and shrimps and succulent bones. He is known as the Brummell of Cats for his elegant well-cut black trousers and spotless white spats!

You can read all about these wonderful cats, including the cat who was once Morgan the pirate but who now acts as the doorkeeper of a publishing house, in *Old Possum's Book of Practical Cats*, by T. S. Eliot, or you could go along to see the musical *Cats* which is based on this book, both of which would be a wonderful treat!

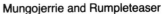

Mungojerrie and Rumpleteaser

Perfect Pancakes

by Julia Nellthorp

illustrated by Susanna Rust

Most of us like pancakes soaked with sugar and lemon juice on Shrove Tuesday but have you ever wondered *why* it is traditional for these delicacies to be served on this day? Pancakes are not a new invention and people have been munching them since the Middle Ages!

The idea of eating pancakes on Shrove Tuesday is linked to the Lent Fast which comes after Shrove Tuesday: traditionally, all the eggs and fats in the house were supposed to be used up before the fast, and pancakes were one very popular way of doing that. Nowadays the Lent Fast is not so widely followed but the pancakes idea has certainly stuck around!

When we think of pancakes the first thing that comes into most of our minds is the 'tossing' of them and the idea of a pancake race complete with bits of batter stuck to floors, ceilings and noses! Well, pancake racing has been around almost as long as pancakes themselves and the first 'race' was an accident: at 11.55 am on Shrove Tuesday in 1445 a housewife in the village of Olney in Buckinghamshire was cooking her pancakes when she heard the bells calling the villagers to church. She was in such a hurry to get to the service that she ran up the hill still carrying her frying pan – with a pancake in it! Olney still has a race on Shrove Tuesday and the competitors now have to toss the pancake once at the start and once at the finish of the 415 yard race.

But pancakes and pancake racing are not confined to Britain, and various types of pancake and races are very popular all over the world. A French Brownie might like crêpes; a German Brownie might prefer pfannkuchen with dried fruit; and in Denmark the batter is often made with beer instead of milk. Some kinds of pancake are very famous – Russian blinis are a small 'posh' pancake served with sour cream and caviar. And you may have heard of Mexican tortillas, Indian chapatis and Israeli blintzes – all these are types of pancakes made with different flours and cooked in different ways. So you see, pancakes are not just our own flat circles served with lemon and sugar; pancakes can be many things and the basic mix of flour, liquid, fat, eggs and seasoning can be made into hundreds of different dishes of many shapes and flavours.

The first thing to get right when you make pancakes is the basic batter. There are lots of different recipes but here is one which will make enough for 12 to 15 pancakes – so you can afford to make one or two mistakes!

Don't forget to wash your hands, tie back your hair and put on an apron before you begin.

Ingredients

4oz/100g plain flour
1 egg
$\frac{1}{2}$ pint/300ml milk
pinch salt

Method

Sieve the flour and salt together into a mixing bowl. Make a well in the middle and add the egg and half of the milk. Stir gently until all the flour is mixed in. Then pour the rest of the milk in and beat with a whisk until the mixture is smooth. Leave the batter for half an hour before you begin cooking.

Cook your pancakes in a frying pan but be very careful not to burn yourself. Melt a very small knob of fat in the pan and gently spoon in one tablespoonful of batter. Don't be tempted to use any more, or the pancakes will turn out more like pan-puddings! Make sure the batter is spread evenly around the pan and then cook for about one minute until the bottom is brownish. Loosen the pancake from the frying pan and turn it over to cook the other side. If you are feeling brave you could toss the pancake instead of just turning it, but try not to drop too many!

Once basic pancakes are made you don't need to limit yourself to lemon and sugar on them – how about honey, cheese, jam, stewed fruit, golden syrup, pâté, cream, chocolate spread, nuts, or baked beans? And you can roll them, fold them into quarters or halves or parcels, or stack them up on top of each other!

The wonderful thing about pancakes is that almost anything goes with them, so why limit yourself to one day a year when you could be tossing and folding any day? Here are some very easy recipes for you to try:

Chocolate Pancakes

1 portion basic pancake mix
½oz/12g cocoa powder
2 tablespoons hot water
double cream and grated chocolate to decorate (optional)

Dissolve the cocoa powder in the water and mix into the batter. Cook as for plain pancakes. Roll and serve with cream and a sprinkle of grated chocolate.

Orange Pancakes

1 portion basic pancake mix
grated rind and juice of one orange
4 fluid oz/120ml whipping cream
6 tablespoons orange marmalade

Whip the cream until it forms stiff peaks, and very gently mix in the orange rind. Keep the cream in the fridge while you cook the pancakes (as for plain pancakes). When each pancake is cooked, spread some marmalade and then a blob of cream on it and roll up before serving – try to serve these pancakes as quickly as you can so that the cream does not melt completely. Perhaps somebody could help you?

Lemon Curd Delights

1 portion basic pancake mix
6 tablespoons lemon curd
4oz/100g vanilla ice cream

Cook the pancakes as for plain pancakes. As each is done, spread a little lemon curd on each and top with a portion of ice cream. Wrap the ice cream like you would a parcel and serve straightaway.

Cream Cheese and Herb Parcels

1 portion basic pancake mix
6oz/150g cream cheese
pinch mixed herbs

Add the mixed herbs to the batter mix. Cook the pancakes in the usual way. As they are cooked put a lump of cream cheese in the middle and gather the pancake up around it. Serve with the neat side facing upwards and decorate with cress if you like.

Mushroom and Stilton Pancakes

1 portion basic pancake mix
6oz/150g grated Stilton cheese (or Cheddar if you prefer)
4oz/100g cooked mushrooms (chopped very small)

Mix half of the cheese and the mushrooms together. Cook the pancakes and keep hot. Divide the cheese and mushroom mix between the pancakes. Spread the mixture over the pancakes and roll them up. Put them in a baking dish and sprinkle the rest of the cheese over them. Brown the pancakes before serving.

Conserve & Save

by Deborah Manley
illustrated by Jane Cope

Conservation is about using the natural resources of the earth wisely and well.

One clause of the Brownie Badge shows how you can save things and use them wisely.

Here are some ideas for you to try. Add three ideas of your own in the space provided. Make sure you try them yourself first!

To make candles burn longer: put them in a freezer for a couple of hours before you use them.

To keep biscuits crisp: put a cube of sugar in the tin with them.

To make rubber bands: cut thin strips from the wrists of worn out rubber gloves before they are thrown away.

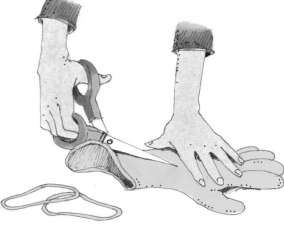

To clean forks: put a dozen milk bottle tops in a jar with a tablespoon of salt and hot water. Dip the forks in the jar while you wash up, then rinse them off.

To loosen sticky tape that's got stuck on the roll: heat it over steam for a few seconds.

To feed your indoor plants: water them with tea left over in the pot.

To give your dog extra nourishment: rinse out the milk bottles and give him the water to drink.

To make bedding for your rabbit: collect crisp, dry autumn leaves.

24

To make garden labels: save your ice lolly sticks.

To make a dibber for planting seeds: use an old pencil.

To have a bubble bath and keep the bath clean: use a mild washing up liquid. It has the same effect as bubble bath and is much cheaper.

To make Christmas tree decorations: collect silver, red and gold tops, wash them carefully and flatten them out. Make stars by cutting slits towards the centre and then twisting the bits round. Make bells by pressing the top down over your finger.

To make outdoor tree decorations for the birds: string popcorn on thread with a needle. Hang the popcorn chains on a tree in the garden for the birds. You could use them on your own tree first and give them to the birds later.

To make a shopping list pad: cut the pictures from old Christmas cards. Punch a hole in one corner. Link them together with string. Use the blank side for the shopping list.

Put your own ideas here after you have tried them out.

FELICIA and the POT of PINKS

illustrated by John Lupton

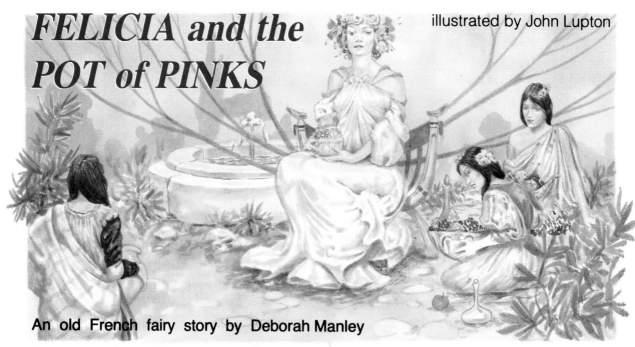

An old French fairy story by Deborah Manley

Once upon a time a poor peasant lived with his two children, Bruno and Felicia, in a little cottage in a great forest. He was old and ill and he called his children to him and said, "Your poor mother brought to our home two stools and a straw bed. I own, too, a hen, a pot of pinks and a silver ring. The ring and the flowers were given to me by a noble lady who once came to our humble home."

He stretched out a feeble hand to point to the pot of pinks where they stood on the window sill. "She said," he went on, "to look after the pinks well and never to forget to water them. She said also, Felicia, that you would grow up to be more beautiful than anyone you saw in your life. When my time came I was to give you the ring and the pot of pinks to console you for your poverty. Take them when I die, Daughter, and Bruno shall have everything else I own."

The old peasant died soon after and Bruno and Felicia divided his possessions, as he had wished. But when Felicia sat down to rest on one of Bruno's stools, he shouted at her, "Get off that stool! It's mine. Keep your pot of pinks and your ring. Leave my things alone."

Felicia was sad, but she loved her brother and did as he said.

When it was supper time Bruno ate one of the hen's fresh eggs. He threw the shell to Felicia. "That's all there is for you," he said. "If you don't like it, go out and catch frogs for your meal."

Felicia went weeping to her little room. It was filled with the sweet scent of the pinks. But she saw that the pot was dry.

She took an old jug and ran to the fountain in the forest. As she approached she saw that a handsome and noble lady was sitting there on a golden sofa. Beautiful maidens served her food from dishes of crystal and silver. The lady wore a crown on her head and Felicia knew she must be the Queen of the Woods.

The Queen looked up and saw Felicia. "Come close, pretty child," she called. "Tell me what you are doing here."

"I came to fetch water for my pot of pinks," said Felicia timidly and held out her jug.

Then she saw that the old, chipped jug had turned to gold, its rim sparkling with diamonds. "Oh, your majesty!" cried Felicia. "Thank you for honouring me so. Let me give you a gift in return. Let me run and get my precious pot of pinks. I wish you to have them."

But when Felicia reached home the pinks were gone. A cabbage lay in their place. "What shall I do?" Felicia asked herself. Then she remembered the silver ring. She ran back with it to the Queen of the Woods.

"Madam," she said, bowing low, "my pot of pinks is gone. Please will you take my silver ring instead?"

"But if I take your ring, my dear, you will have nothing left."

"If I have your friendship," replied Felicia, "I will do very well."

The Queen slipped the ring onto her finger. She thanked Felicia and then mounted her chariot. It was decorated with coral and emeralds and was drawn by six milk-white horses.

Felicia watched the Queen and her maidens until they disappeared among the trees. Then she went slowly back through the forest, thinking of all the spendid things she had seen.

When she woke in the morning, the first thing she saw was the cabbage. She jumped up and was about to kick it when she heard it speak.

"Don't hurt me!" cried the cabbage.

Felicia drew back in fear.

The cabbage went on in a kindly voice. "Take me, dear girl, and plant me with my comrades in the garden. Then find your pinks. They are in Bruno's room, for he took them and left me here in their place."

Felicia overcame her fear. She took the cabbage and planted it in the garden. Just then Bruno's hen went by, clucking and pecking at the ground. Felicia grabbed it.

"You horrid creature!" she cried. "I shall

punish you for my brother's wickedness."

"No, no!" clucked the hen. "Don't hurt me. Listen, for I am a great gossip. I know many secrets. Hear what I have to tell."

Felicia was amazed to hear the hen speak. She held her gently now and listened to her tale. "You are not a poor peasant's daughter," said the hen. "Your mother was a queen. She had six daughters already and her husband, the king, threatened that, unless she had a son to inherit his kingdom, he would cut off her head."

"So what did she do?" asked Felicia.

"She arranged with her friend, who was a fairy, to exchange you for the fairy's little son. But, when you were born, the fairy did not send her son. So your mother escaped from the palace with you in her arms. She wandered in the forest until she reached this cottage. She gave you to the peasant's wife. Then she died."

"How sad," whispered Felicia, with tears in her eyes.

"I was that peasant woman," said the hen.

"You!" exclaimed Felicia.

"Yes, I. But I was also a gossip. I told my tale to the neighbours. Then one day a beautiful lady came from the forest. I told her my tale, too, gossip that I was. Then she waved her wand and I became the hen that you see. That, until today, was the end of my gossiping."

"What happened then?" asked Felicia.

"My poor husband looked everywhere for me. He decided that I must have been killed by wild beasts in the forest. Then the lady came again. She gave him a silver ring and a pot of pinks."

"My ring and my pinks," murmured Felicia.

"Then the King sent soldiers to search for you," the hen went on. "The lady turned them into those cabbages with her wand."

"And now they too can speak," said Felicia in wonder.

"Never before today," said the hen. "I think that some great thing is about to happen."

"I hope it will, dear hen. I leave you now. I must go to search for my pot of pinks."

Bruno had gone out into the forest. The cottage was empty. Felicia slipped into his room and saw her pot of pinks on the straw bed. But there, guarding them, was a horrible army of rats. They sprang at her, screeching and scratching, their teeth yellow and sharp.

Felicia drew back. How can I rescue my pot of pinks? she wondered. Then she thought of the golden pitcher. Perhaps it is magical as well as beautiful, she thought. And sure enough it was. She sprinkled water from it over the rats. They vanished at once. Not a whisker, nor a tail, nor one of their gnashing teeth remained.

The poor pinks were dry and wilting. Felicia scattered the last drops of water from the jug over them. She bent down to breathe in their delicious scent.

Then a quiet voice seemed to rustle among the leaves.

"Lovely, Felicia, the day has come when I can

tell you that even the flowers adore your beauty."

The pinks were speaking !

It was too much for Felicia, she sank to the floor in a faint.

Bruno found her there, lying on the floor of his room. He was furious that she had found the pinks. He dragged her out of the house and left her on the hard ground.

Slowly the air revived Felicia. She opened her eyes. There before her stood the Queen of the Woods.

"I shall punish your cruel brother for this," the Queen said angrily.

"Do not, dear Queen. I am not angry with him for he is my brother."

"But if he were not your brother would you not then be angry?" asked the Queen.

"How could it be that he is not my brother?" asked Felicia.

"You have been told, Felicia, that you are really a princess. Did you not believe the hen's story?"

"How could I believe that, your majesty, with no real proof?"

At that moment a very handsome young man came towards them. He was dressed all in green velvet and wore a crown of pinks on his head.

"My son!" cried the Queen. "You are returned to human form at last." She held him close to her. "Let me explain," she said, turning to Felicia. "Long ago I promised to send my son to my friend the Queen in exchange for her baby girl. On the way a bad fairy turned him into a pot of pinks. There was only one way he could be returned to human form. I brought him to you,

hoping that your love would bring him back. And so it has now happened."

The Queen and Prince Pink smiled happily at Felicia. Shyly, she smiled back.

"Do you think, dear girl, that you could love my son enough to marry him?" asked the Queen.

Felicia looked at the handsome young man and knew that she could love him. "Yes," she said, "that would make me very happy."

"You shall be married here, with the silver ring," said the Queen, "but first you must be dressed as befits your rank."

She touched Felicia with her wand and Felicia's ragged dress became a magnificent robe embroidered with pearls, and a golden coronet encircled her head.

Prince Pink held out his hand to her. At that moment Bruno came back from the forest. He could hardly believe his eyes. What was his sister doing dressed so grandly and with such noble people?

Felicia called him to her. "Please be kind to Bruno," she begged the Queen.

"What! You ask for this, though he has been so cruel?" The Queen was amazed.

"I am so happy," said Felicia, "I want everyone to be happy."

So the Queen turned the cottage into a splendid palace, richly furnished. "But," she said, "your two stools and your straw bed will always be there to remind you where you came from."

With another wave of her wand, she returned the hen and the cabbages to their human forms. And so everyone lived happily ever after, but Felicia and her prince were happiest of all.

BRITAIN'S PATRON SAINTS

by Susan Tyte   illustrated by David Brian

The United Kingdom of Great Britain is represented by the Union Flag. Those words 'united' and 'union' mean joined together to make one. Our country is really four small countries which have come together to make one larger country. Each of those countries has its own special saint.

Their flags have been put together to form our Union Flag. Read the stories below and find out about the four saints. Then try to find their section of the Union Flag.

Saint George of England

In a far-off country was a small town where the people lived in great fear. Close to the town was a misty swamp where a fearsome dragon lived.

This monster ate sheep and cattle as they grazed, chased townfolk and scorched the town walls with its fiery breath. Any unfortunate caught in the dragon's sharp claws was dragged off to its dark lair.

Desperate to save themselves from this terror, the townspeople made a plan. They would offer the monster their princess, in the hope that this would keep them from being harmed.

So the poor girl was taken outside, tied to a rock, and left for the dragon. Riding through the countryside at this time, was a brave knight called George. On his arm he carried a white shield with a red cross and in his hand he held a sword. Suddenly he heard crashing and roaring! His horse reared with fright. Through the raging, George heard crying.

Wheeling his horse around, he galloped towards the commotion, and found himself facing a huge, coiling monster and a terrified girl. Swinging his sword through the air, George forced it down on the dragon's neck. The monster turned. George cut again. With a gasp of fire and steam the monster fell back, dragging itself off to its swamp.

George untied the girl and together they rode back to the town. The people were amazed to see their princess unharmed, and gratefully thanked the courageous knight. They were never again troubled by the dragon.

English people enjoyed this story so much that they chose George as their own saint, and his red cross on a white background as their banner.

Saint Andrew of Scotland

Andrew is the only one of Britain's saints whose story is told in the Bible.

Jesus was just beginning his travels around Palestine, telling the people about God's love for them, when he chose twelve special friends to come with him.

Andrew was working with his brother Simon by the Lake of Galilee. They were fishermen, mending their nets, having just come ashore with another day's catch of fish. Busily working they did not see the stranger walking along the shore. But they heard him call out to them, "Come with me. I will teach you to catch men instead of fish!" Hardly knowing why, Andrew and Simon left their nets and, hurrying along the water's edge, caught up with the man called Jesus.

One day, a huge crowd followed Jesus to hear him talk. As the day wore on, the people got hungry. It occured to them that they had had nothing to eat. A young boy came up to Andrew and said, "I have five loaves of bread and two fish; you can share them out, but they won't feed everyone here." Andrew took the boy to Jesus, and explained the problem.

Jesus thanked God for the food and began to give it to the people. Instead of it running out, there was enough for everyone, and even enough left over to fill twelve baskets. Andrew stayed with Jesus until his Lord was killed on a cross.

Jesus was dead but Andrew worked on. He travelled great distances telling everyone he met about Jesus. Through his teaching many became Christians.

But the early followers of Jesus were unpopular with the authorities. When he was an old man, Andrew was arrested and hung on an 'X' shape cross to die.

Scottish people chose Andrew as their saint. His white cross on a blue background is their flag.

Saint Patrick of Ireland

Many hundreds of years ago, a boy called Patrick enjoyed the stories about Jesus that his mother told him. She taught him how to pray as well.

Patrick had a happy life. One day he was playing on the beach. Fierce shouts and clattering swords suddenly interrrupted the game: it was a pirate raid! Patrick was snatched and dragged off to the boats which set sail at once.

He was taken across the sea to Ireland. Here he was sold to a chief and set to work as a slave. It was his task to look after the cattle and pigs. Often he was lonely out in the fields, but he remembered to say his prayers and reminded himself of the stories about Jesus he had learnt from his mother.

For six long years, Patrick was enslaved. Eventually he escaped, and travelled to the coast. There he found some boats getting ready to sail. He begged to be allowed aboard and the sailors took pity on him.

Setting sail, they headed for Britain. But a storm blew them across the water to France. Patrick stayed there for many years. During this time he learned more about Jesus and the Bible. Then he returned to Britain and was reunited with his family.

But in his heart, Patrick knew that God wanted him to return to Ireland, to teach the people there about Jesus. So again, he set sail. When he reached land he began travelling the country, talking about God's care and baptizing many. The people loved him and rushed to meet him wherever he went. Churches were built and many became Christians because of him.

Patrick lived to be an old man. He is remembered by a red diagonal cross on a white background.

Saint David of Wales

Fourteen hundred years ago, in the part of Britain called Wales, lived a man called David. He was a royal prince, rich and powerful. But David had no liking for money and worldly affairs. He wanted to spend his life working for God. So he went to study with the most famous teacher of the time, a man called Paulinus.

Having stayed with Paulinus for many years, David began journeying around Wales, telling the people about Jesus.

Travelling through the hills and valleys of Wales was often difficult, and sometimes dangerous. Sometimes David went on foot, sometimes he rode a pony. Nothing stopped his work and the Welsh people loved and respected him.

With the help of those he had introduced to Christianity, David founded a great church near the sea. Today that place has been named Saint Davids in the memory of him.

David lived to be about seventy years old – a great age for those times.

Saint David does not have his own flag, and the Welsh banner showing a red dragon on a white and green background is not on the Union flag. But the Welsh are proud of their saint. On his special day, many wear a bright yellow daffodil, like a brooch, to show that they remember their Saint David.

REMEMBER OUR SAINTS' DAYS

Wales ~ St. David, March 1st.

Ireland ~ St. Patrick, March 17th.

England ~ St. George, April 23rd.

Scotland ~ St. Andrew, November 30th.

Your own Miniature Farmyard

By Anne Moffat

You can make your own miniature farmyard from these two pages, just by cutting out all the pieces, folding and sticking them together.

All you need is some lightweight card, paper, glue and scissors.

1. First cut out the barn and the yard, following the outline. Stick onto the card. If you have no spare card, use an old cereal box instead; it will do just as well.

2. When the glue has dried, carefully cut round the edges of the barn and yard; don't cut the flaps off!

3. Fold the barn up along the dotted lines, folding the sides of the barn backwards and the roof and rear wall towards the back.

4. Fold the flaps back and glue onto the sides and roof.

5. When dry, cut small slots in the front wall, (*marked on diagram) to slot the tabs of the field into.

6. If you want the barn/stable doors to open, cut along the opening side of the door and across the top, folding doors open where the hinges are on a real door.

7. Now fold up the walls joining the field, to make a front and back to each wall.

8. Take the wall with the gate on it and fold the tabs back. Bend the flap back and glue onto the underneath of the yard; let it dry.

9. Glue between the side walls, stick them together and before the glue dries, slot the two tabs on the gate wall between the side walls to make a square solid wall for the yard.

10. Fold up and glue the back flap of the yard onto the inside front of the barn and slot tabs into the edges of the barn.

FOLD

FOLD

FOLD

FOLD

FOLD

FOLD

FOLD

FOLD

FOLD   *CUT SLOT

FOLD   *CUT SLOT

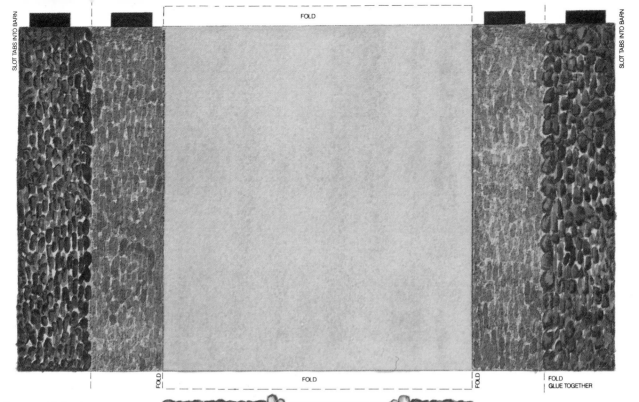

FOLD

FOLD

FOLD

FOLD

FOLD

FOLD
GLUE TOGETHER

Trees and Animals

(these don't need sticking onto card).

Cut the animals out around their outline and the green base. Fold the base upwards so they are at right angles to the animal. Glue the backs and fronts of the animals together; do not glue the bases. Stand the animals in your farmyard.

FOLD TABS OUT

Cut out the trees and glue fronts to backs. Before they dry, slip over each side of one of the walls, so that you can see the tree on both sides. Put the trees wherever you want in the farmyard.

GLUE TOGETHER

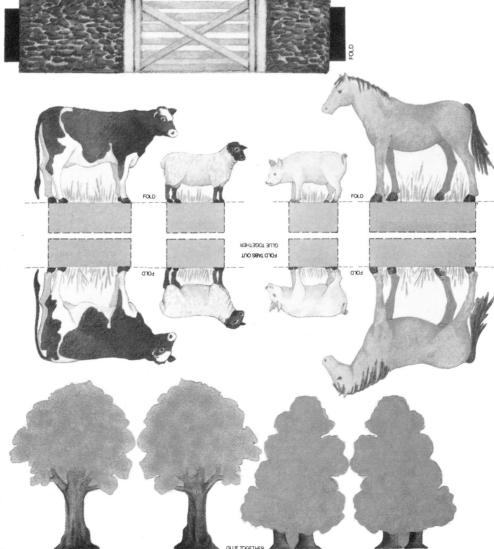

FOLD

FOLD

FOLD TABS OUT   GLUE TOGETHER

FOLD

FOLD

GLUE TOGETHER

33

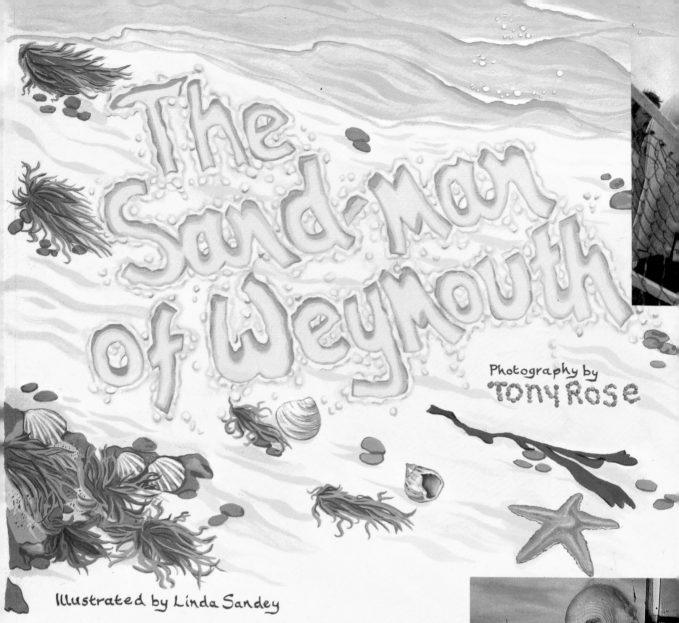

The Sand-Man of Weymouth

Photography by TONY ROSE

Illustrated by Linda Sandey

You may already have seen Fred Darrington's work on television – it has appeared on Blue Peter, Get Fresh and T.V. AM, to name only a few programmes. If you have, you'll know that he's probably Britain's most famous 'sand sculptor'.

Although he doesn't build sandcastles, he does make just about everything else, as you can see from the pictures on the next few pages, taken when I visited him in Weymouth recently.

Fred's career in sand began many years ago, when, as a boy, he used to make elaborate models in sand as a way of earning sweet money from passers-by (Fred has a very sweet tooth). One of his most popular models in those days was of a house with a smoking chimney, which was made by putting a lighted piece of rag inside the hollowed-out shape.

Today, his models are even more ambitious, and are often inspired by important events, or famous people. All the designs are original – Fred does not copy them from anywhere else, and once he has decided on a subject, he doesn't usually need to make any drawings of it first.

Fred works a 12 to 15 hour day at the height of the summer season. He doesn't have time to stop for meals, and so he makes mugs of tea and eats biscuits as he works.

Not surprisingly, people get to know about Fred's sand sculptures and stop to look. Other passers-by wonder what's going on ... and so the crowd grows.

The sand Fred uses comes from Portland stone and is easily modelled when combined with water. In fact, Fred's completed models will usually last up to about three weeks, provided that the weather remains good (wind and heavy rain would damage them).

I'd expected Fred to have a lot of expensive modelling tools, but instead, he only had a variety of things which would be found in most kitchens – table knives, a palette knife for smoothing rough surfaces, spoons and a brush to remove any unwanted sand.

Fred agreed to make a special sculpture in honour of our visit – a Brownie owl on a Guide Trefoil. The pictures below show how this was done.

Fred works quickly, mixing sand with water to form up a big block of sand. Using a spoon, he carves away some of the sand to make a rough owl shape, and then with a knife, he puts in details, such as eyes, beak and feathers.

After this, he smooths the surface of the remaining block of sand with a palette knife, and draws in the outline of the Trefoil badge with the point of a kitchen knife.

This done, he starts to carve out the shape, brushing away surplus sand as he goes.
He scoops out each 'petal' of the Trefoil.

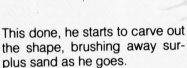

Next, the details are put in. This takes quite a while — all the unwanted sand has to be brushed away very carefully so that the design isn't damaged.

Lastly, Fred puts in the scroll below the Trefoil, and carves the motto 'Be Prepared'. The sculpture now *looks* finished – but Fred has other ideas!

He mixes some water and white powder paint in a bucket, and using a coarse brush, coats the sculpture with it.

Then, using yellow, black and brown colours, he paints the owl, making it seem much more realistic.

The finishing touch is a spray of gold aerosol paint.

The completed owl and Trefoil. Well done Fred!

Muffin

by Sheila Payne

illustrated by Jane Cope

Melanie could not get out of school fast enough that Friday afternoon. She was irritable and cross and near to tears. She threw her coat on, grabbed her bag, and was off.

"Bye, Mel. See you Monday," someone called after her.

But she did not answer, or slow down, until she was through the school gates and walking up the High Street.

The first week of term after the summer had been awful. Everyone was talking about their holidays, and showing their photographs. And even today after storytime, when Mrs Graham had asked for news, Bob and Anna had got up and told the class about their camping trip to France.

It was just too much, when she had not been away at all. She knew she wasn't the only one whose father was out of work and the family short of money. Carol's father hadn't a job, either. Nor had John's. Only John had been to stay with his Nan by the sea.

She didn't know quite why she was so fed up. The holidays had been fun. It was just that nothing she had done seemed like 'news' beside the others' adventures. She couldn't join in. It was a sort of loneliness.

So when she found the little scared cat, mewing in the lane by the waste ground on her way home, she thought she knew how it felt.

She tried to stroke it, but it backed away, frightened. Its long black and white fur was matted with mud and stuck with burs.

Melanie remembered she had not finished her lunch. She broke up half a cheese sandwich on the ground and stood back a bit. The cat ate greedily, looking wildly at Melanie between mouthfuls.

It was so bedraggled and seemed lost. She wanted to take it home with her. But when she tried to hold it, it was impossible. It struggled so.

If she ran all the way she could get a box and be back in a few minutes. But would it still be there...

She could not think what else to do, but as she ran it followed her. She could see it through the bushes, the flash of white through the leaves, keeping up with her.

When she came to the busy road at the end of the lane, the cat stopped. Melanie came back to it and managed this time, very gently, to pick it up, and tuck it inside her coat.

"That you, Mel?" her mother called from the kitchen.

The cat was struggling desperately in Melanie's arms at the sound of a strange voice.

"What have you got there?" said Mother.

As if in answer, the cat leaped out from under Melanie's coat, landed on the rug in front of the boiler, and ran under a chair.

"It's a stray," said Melanie.

"Are you sure?"

"I found it in the lane. It's ever so hungry."

Her mother knelt on the floor to take a closer look. "Oh, the poor little thing."

"Can we keep it?" Melanie asked. "Please Mum."

"Oh, Mel." Mother put her arms round Melanie and was about to say that they could not afford it. But she was suddenly so tired of saying that, and seeing Melanie's disappointment, she said, "Oh, Mel, what a good idea," instead. Which surprised both of them so much they looked at each other and laughed.

They got a tin of sardines out of the store

cupboard for its supper. And Melanie chose from the pile of odd crockery on the dresser her favourite yellow saucer with pink flowers on, and a blue plate with a fine gold line round the edge.

"Well, it's certainly going to eat in style," said Mother.

It ate the sardines and drank some milk, and even let Melanie stroke it a bit, though it went back under the chair again – just in case.

Melanie's father came in late. He had spent half the day travelling to a neighbouring town where he had heard there was a job.

"How did it go?" asked Mother.

He shook his head. He sat down in the kitchen and took off his shoes.

"Eighty others after it. What chance is there?"

He was tired and dispirited. And when he heard about the cat he was angry.

"Goodness woman, we can hardly feed ourselves," he shouted.

Melanie knew when her father said 'Goodness woman' to Mum he was very cross indeed.

But his temper was like a firework rocket – it flared up and was over just as quickly. In a few moments, he said, "Let's have a look at it then," and bent down to see under the chair.

Melanie looked at her mother and grinned. Her mother smiled and ruffled Father's hair.

"Come and have your supper," she said.

Later, Father said he would take a walk down to the flats over the shops backing onto the lane, to see if the cat belonged to anyone there.

"Someone might be looking for it, Mel," he said as she protested.

Melanie went to bed, but she could not sleep till he came back. He popped his head round her bedroom door.

"No one knows anything about it," he said.

Saturday morning, Melanie and her mother took the cat to the vet. Mother said what about the expense, but Father insisted. If they were going to keep the cat, they must make sure it was all right. For its own sake and theirs.

The cat was quiet in the vet's hands, crouched on the shiny white table under the bright light. Melanie waited anxiously by her mother, as the vet felt the cat all over, and looked in its eyes and ears and mouth. The light was very warm and the white of the table dazzling.

"She's fine," he said, at last. "Needs feeding up though." He turned to get some scissors to cut away some of the matted fur. "If she's going to have healthy kittens," he added.

"Kittens!" said Melanie and her mother together.

"Kittens," he repeated. "Didn't you know? Quite soon."

Melanie was so excited. When they got home, she let the cat out of the basket just inside the front door, and ran through to the garden where her father was tying up the tall, golden rod flowering in the autumn sunshine.

"It's a girl, and she's going to have kittens, and I'm going to call her Muffin," she said, jumping up and down.

(She had decided to call her Muffin on the bus coming home. It would be short for Ragamuffin, which she looked like, but not so rude – that would be their loving secret, her's and Muffin's.)

"Never rains but it pours," said Father to Mother, who had followed Melanie out into the garden.

Melanie looked up at them both. "Aren't you excited?" she said. But she did not wait for their answer, because she was so very excited herself.

She ran off up the garden again, and into the house to find Muffin.

She ran upstairs and tipped her money box out over her bed. She had been saving up to have her ears pierced, like Anna's. She had one pound sixty.

She went down to the pet shop straightaway and bought a brush, and a bright red ball with a bell in it, which tinkled when you rolled it.

Muffin was eating well, and beginning to clean herself up. She refused to sit in the box prepared for her, like any self-respecting cat, preferring to curl up on the armchair by the boiler, or on Melanie's lap (whenever she would sit still).

Melanie rushed home from school every day to play with her and cuddle her. She would lean over the bannisters in her nightie whispering, "Muffin, Muffin", to entice her upstairs to sleep on her bed (much against her mother's wishes), while her parents were watching television.

About two weeks after Muffin arrived, they heard that the factory in the town was closing down. There would be more people out of work. It would be harder than ever for Father to get a job. Mother talked of getting another morning's cleaning work to help out. They both sounded very worried.

Melanie sat in her bedroom, looking at her almost empty money box, regretting her extravagance. She could have used her doll's brush for Muffin really, and bought some tins of cat food instead. She couldn't quite regret the red ball. And Muffin loved it.

How could she earn enough money to feed Muffin? The boys next door cleaned cars. But they were bigger than her. She wouldn't be able to reach the top, unless she stood on something.

She slept on the idea and in the morning had a better one. If *she* couldn't think what to do, perhaps other people might.

She carefully copied out several times on stiff coloured paper:

> *Any small job done*
> *e.g. car cleaning.*
> *Contact Melanie Johnson.*

and cut it up into separate cards.

She hoped 'e.g. car cleaning' would be all right. Some cars were small. Mrs Graham had a small car... Melanie put one of her cards on her teacher's desk. The rest she put through their neighbours' letter boxes.

And waited.

The first reaction was from Mother, who had met several of the neighbours out shopping. She was cross because she had not known about it, and sad because she did not want Melanie to feel worried about money. She was worried because she did not want Melanie to be tired and not attending to her school work, but she was proud of her as well, which was a difficult mixture of feelings.

Father was worried for her safety. But he understood her wanting to look after Muffin.

"You're not going doing things for any strangers," he said. "Or taking on anything too hard. Talk about Muffin," he said, encircling Melanie in his arms. "You're only a small thing yourself."

"Mrs Graham says I can clean her car for fifty pence a week," said Melanie by way of answer, disengaging herself, because she felt more grown up than they were saying.

Melanie was right. Other people thought of all sorts of things she could do. In the next few days, as well as cleaning Mrs Graham's car, she did some shopping for one neighbour, weeded another one's front path and took another's dog for a walk.

When she went with Mother to the supermarket Friday night, she had more than enough for Muffin's food.

When they came home, Muffin was very restless. "She's looking for somewhere to have her kittens," said Mother.

By morning they were born, three of them, on a pile of dusters in the cupboard under the stairs. Melanie watched as Muffin fed them, purring contentedly. There was one black one (who had its mother's long fur) and two black and white ones.

Muffin was very busy for the next few weeks, staying in the warm kitchen, looking after her family. She needed plenty of food while she was feeding her kittens, and Melanie worked hard to earn the money (when she was not playing with them all). She could not always earn enough, and then Mother would help out, but mostly she managed.

When the kittens began their staggering exploration of the kitchen, then the hall, and then the sitting-room, and to be interested in the red ball, Mother said, "We shall have to find homes for them soon."

Still Father was out of work. When Mother talked of finding the kittens homes, he said, "Well, let's hope it's not as difficult as me finding a job." It sounded like a joke, and her father was trying to smile, but Melanie knew he was miserable.

"You'll find something soon," said Mother, but she did not sound very convincing, either.

The kittens grew bigger, and began to be more independent of Muffin. She did not feed them so much, or seem to worry so much where they were. They began to eat porridge and bits of minced meat.

For the same reason Father had been cross at first about Muffin, it was not going to be easy, now the factory had closed, to find homes for them.

It was difficult to let them go, too. When you had watched them growing and played with them, and knew their ways, it was difficult to agree that anyone was going to be able to look after them well enough. Or had the right sort of home.

"They mustn't be too near a main road," said Mother.

"And they must have a garden," said Melanie.

And we must like the look of them, they both thought to themselves.

The little black she kitten went to Anna and Bob with no trouble. But the two black and white boy kittens just stuck. One was promised a home and then the people changed their minds. One was wanted as a birthday present for someone's granddaughter, and then they found she had an allergy to animal fur. And so it went on.

There was one disastrous morning when a woman with a very shrill voice came to look at the kittens. They had had great hopes of this one. She had said on the phone she just *loved* animals. Father had said, "Now don't let this one get away," before he went out to buy a paper.

But when they heard her, first one kitten, and then the other following fast, crept out of the room, belly to the ground and ears flattened. It was rather embarrassing. The woman left in a bit of a huff.

"They didn't like her," said Melanie.

"No, they didn't. But I don't know quite how we're going to explain that to your father."

"They soon won't be kittens anymore and then it'll be harder still to find homes for them," said Father. "We *cannot* keep them," he added,

looking firmly at Melanie, who could not truthfully say the thought had not crossed her mind. So she said nothing.

Muffin was sitting on the armchair by the boiler.

"And I don't want that cat sitting on my chair, either," he said, shooing Muffin off.

"Dad doesn't mean to be grumpy. He's just very worried," said Mother, later. "But try and keep Muffin off that chair."

Melanie was busy getting ready to go out on one of her jobs. Although it was a few weeks to Christmas, she was going to help old Mrs Bromford write her cards. Mrs Bromford was nearly blind and she had asked Melanie to write the envelopes for her.

"She's not paying you for that, is she?" said Mother.

Melanie fidgeted, looking at her best pen.

"Mel, you are not taking money for helping old Mrs B. We're not that hard up."

"But Mum."

"Absolutely no."

Melanie went off up the road feeling it was going to be a wasted afternoon. But she liked Mrs B. and actually enjoyed writing the addresses in her best handwriting.

Mrs B. said it had helped her enormously and if Melanie wouldn't take any money, then she must stay and have a drink of orange juice and a piece of her home-made fruit cake. So it was that while Melanie was eating she told Mrs B. all about the kittens.

"My nephew was talking about getting a kitten, or was it a puppy, for his little girl," said Mrs B. "I'll mention it to him. He's probably coming over tomorrow."

Sunday morning there was a knock at the door. It was Mrs. B's nephew. He had a bright ginger beard, and a smiling face, and spoke quickly in little bursts.

"My aunt tells me you've got a kitten – ah, there it is," he said, as one of the kittens sidled up to him, and wound round his legs. "Let's have a look at you," he said picking him up. The kitten purred.

Melanie and her mother looked at each other.

"Come in," said Father.

"Yes, come in," said Mother taking him into the sitting-room.

They were soon joined by the other kitten who was rarely far from his brother.

"Two of them!" said Mrs B.'s nephew.

One kitten bent its head to let the other wash its ears.

"Pity to separate them," said Mrs B.'s nephew.

They tumbled over together playing.

"I'd like them both, if that's all right," said Mrs B.'s nephew.

Melanie and her mother scrambled out into the kitchen delighted, and prepared the kittens' box for the journey. They lined it with fresh paper and an old jumper Melanie had grown out of.

They heard Mrs B.'s nephew talking to Father. And like people often do, he said, "What do you do?"

"I'm out of work at the moment," said Father.

"Oh, I'm sorry. Were you at the factory that just closed?"

"No. I was working over at Marlowe's. Deliveries and stock records."

"It's a year since they closed."

"'Fraid so."

There was a pause.

"I manage Dewbury's, the furniture place out on the bypass," said Mrs B.'s nephew. "I shall need a new storekeeper at the warehouse after Christmas. Interested?"

"Yes. Yes, I am."

"Well, here's my business card. Come over and have a talk with me about it tomorrow. Ten o'clock all right? I can show you round."

"Yes, of course."

He turned to Melanie at the door. "We don't live far away. You can come and see the kittens some time."

And off he went.

They shut the front door, and the house seemed very quiet for a moment.

Then Father let out a great whoop of joy, and hugged Mother and Melanie, and whirled them round together in the hall till they were all dizzy.

"Who would have thought that," said Mother, "when we woke up this morning."

"It's all Muffin's doing," said Melanie. And they went to tell her what a clever girl she was.

Muffin was standing in the middle of the kitchen floor. She looked at them, and stretched and yawned. Then she walked over to the armchair by the boiler. She jumped lightly onto the seat, turned round three times, curled up and went to sleep.

You will need:-

Lightweight card (like that used to make greetings cards)
Scissors
Slit pin
Glue
Felt tip pens or crayons

BUSY BETSY BROWNIE!

by Kim Collins

To make the model of Betsy the Busy Brownie you must cut out the page opposite and paste it on to the light card. (If you do not want to cut this page out of your annual you can carefully trace out the design and copy it on to the light card, then colour it in yourself.)

Cut out the whole picture of Betsy along the thick black lines, including the white tabs, then fold Betsy in half along the dotted lines on her woolly hat. Make two holes where the black dots are on her dress.

Now cut out the legs piece and make a hole in the middle where the black dot is.

Slot the legs between the two halves of Betsy and push the slit pin through all the three holes that you have made, flattening it out on the other side to keep the model secure.

Hold the white tabs and gently push the model along on a flat surface and see Betsy the Busy Brownie bustle along.

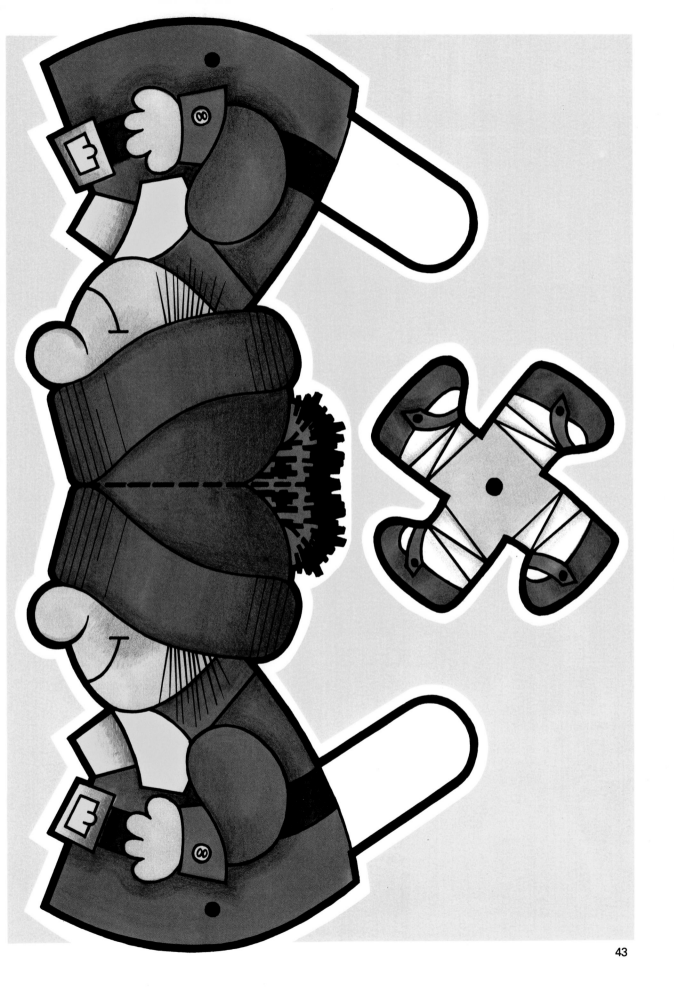

BROWNIES on skids!

Photographs by Christopher Phillips

It was an exciting day for the 60th (All Saints) Rhiwbina Brownies, when they arrived at the Bridgend Police Headquarters, Mid-Glamorgan, for a visit to the Police Museum and nearby skid pan.

I had been invited to join them, by their Brown Owl, Mrs Jenny Legge, and was as pleased as the Brownies were, to be coming on such an unusual expedition.

Sergeant David Lewis met us at Police Headquarters, and introduced us to Sergeant Reg Dodson, who has been Curator at the Museum for the past fifteen

It's difficult reaching the pedals of a Panda car when you're Brownie-size.

Here you can see part of Sergeant Dodson's collection of caps.

years. (A curator looks after the exhibits in a museum, acquires new ones when possible and explains the collection to visitors.)

He told us that the Museum was founded in 1907, (by a Mr E. R. Baker, who later became the Deputy Chief Constable of Glamorgan), ever since then it has been growing in size, as items have been gradually added to the collection.

The oldest exhibit is an entire police cell, complete with barred window, which dates from 1845. A couple of brave Brownies actually went inside, but seemed quite glad to be let out later on!

Another reconstructed item was the Day Rest Room, dating from 1900. It was the place where all the police officers at a station would have spent their free time, before and after shifts. There was a big table, and bench seats, but no television or radio, of course.

This car was not likely to go anywhere (it only had two wheels and half a body!).

Police motorbikes are very big. They need to have large engines so that they can go fast.

A spin on the skid pan is obviously very giggle-making!

Soon our visit was over and we climbed back into our coach for the trip to the skid pan.

Here we were met by Chief Inspector Clive Wynne Hughes, and were shown the model engine room. It was fascinating to see real cars and motorbikes displayed so that it was clear how all the different parts of the engines worked. We could even get inside and 'drive' a car sawn lengthwise!

The police motorbike rider training area was our next stop. We were allowed to get on the bikes and try them out for size. Getting off them was slightly harder, as they were so big! From the photographs, it seems that some of the Brownies plan future careers as bike outriders!

The real excitement of the day was a 'spin' on the skid pan. From the photograph you can see that this experience was a lot of fun.

All too soon, it was time to go, and after a Brownie 'Thank You' to the staff at the skid pan and museum, it was time to get back into our coach for the return journey after a day spent in 'police custody'!

The Brownie Annual would like to thank Sergeants David Lewis and Reg Dodson and all the staff at Bridgend Police Headquarters and the South Wales Constabulary Driving School for their help in organising this visit.

After a Brownie 'Thank You' for the staff of the Police Driving School, everybody poses for a photograph.

We wondered how those policemen of long ago passed their spare time. Perhaps, by reading, or playing cards or dominoes, but certainly not by watching TV!

Next, we looked at the Museum's international collection of uniforms. Some of the Brownies tried out American police shirts for size — rather too big for comfort.

Sergeant Dodson also had a huge collection of police hats which had been sent in by police forces from all over the world.

Again, not very many of these could be described as a good fit, on the Brownies' heads.

STITCHES TO SEND.

Do you keep the cards people send you at Christmas and Birthday times? Sometimes they are so funny or lovely to look at, that it is a pity ever to throw them away. The cards on these pages are rather like that, most people would be glad to be sent one!

By Linda Sandey

Happy Easter

1/ Cut two ovals of fabric and stitch together leaving the top open.

2/ Sew ribbon around the middle of the egg, tie in a bow at the front.

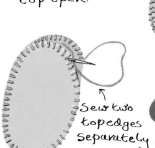

Sew two top edges separately

3/ Cut smaller ovals of fabric to hold needles and pins, place inside egg.

Happy Mothers ~ Day ~

1/ Fold a large piece of blue card in half.

2/ Cut a piece of green fabric to fit the front of the folded card, and lightly trace the message which you want to send.

3/ Embroider using any kind of stitch you like and glue to the front of the card.

4/ Cut an aeroplane shape out of foil and glue to the top of the card.

5/ White tissue paper makes an aeroplane trail, and cotton wool makes good clouds.

Cut the top into the shape you want

46

Happy Birthday

1, Cut the clown's head out of white fabric.

2, Cut the eyebrows and mouth from contrasting fabric and stitch in place.

3, A button makes a good nose.

Embroider eyes.

4, Cut a bow-tie from brightly coloured material and glue in place.

cut loops

To make hair thread fine wool through the top of the head in loops.

To finish back the head onto a piece of stiff card.

Merry Xmas

1, Draw the figure onto a piece of stiff pink card and cut out.

Cut tabs at a slight angle

Fold back tabs

2, From red fabric cut a hat and coat.

3, Using black fabric cut a belt and some boots and stitch in place on the coat.

4, Glue the hat and coat to the figure.

5, Cut two semi-circles of pink card for hands.

6, With felt pens draw on the face, finish with cotton wool for a beard.

Congratulations for a new ~baby~

1, Fill a small envelope with dried rice or lentils and tape to the centre of a long piece of card.

2, Fold one end of the card to the middle and stick in place.

3, Cut a circle of pink paper to make the baby's face and edge with lace.

Finish with a pink or blue bow.

The Private Life of the Robin

written and photographed by Michael Edwards

Illustrated by Tony Rose

I was digging over my garden border before the first winter frosts turned the soil into pre-cast concrete, when there was a flurry of wings at my feet.

I turned to see a cheeky robin swallowing a fat worm he had snatched from between the prongs of my garden fork. He looked sleek and colourful in the pale winter sun, as though he had just fallen from a Christmas card.

The sending of greetings cards began in Victorian times and the much loved robin was a natural choice of the designers.

The robin's Christmas popularity stems from the legend that a bird attempted to remove the sharp thorns from the head of Jesus at the Crucifixion. A drop of blood fell on the bird's chest and forever after, the robin wore a red 'bib'. The bird decorated not only Christmas cards, but valentines too. Even the red-uniformed postmen of the time were nicknamed 'robins'.

In 1961, following a proposal by the International Council for Bird Protection that every member country should adopt a representative bird, the lovable robin was chosen as our national bird.

Although the robin is a typical garden bird in Britain, over most of Europe it is a woodland bird, shy and wary of human beings, and quite unlike the redbreast we know and love.

But for the robin, our gardens would be in silence during the autumn and winter, for unlike other birds, robins continue to sing at this time.

After a couple of weeks rest in early December, the song strikes up again and continues until mid-July. Between then and mid-July

48

the robin moults (loses a lot of feathers) and is silent.

Like the song of most small birds, that of the robin contains high-frequency notes which we cannot hear. In autumn, it sings a different song. It is sung very softly and is not audible to human ears at a distance of more than a few feet. As sweet and pleasant as it is, the robin's autumn song is still thought of as unlucky by some elderly country people. In some areas, to allow a robin into a house was to risk disaster, even death. It was especially upsetting for a sick person to hear a robin sing.

Bird song is produced by air vibration, just as it is in many

A typical garden habitat of the robin.

A robin tends its chicks in their nest built on my garage shelf.

musical instruments. Song is a form of warning in which a bird tells others to keep away from its territory. Even in winter, unlike other garden birds, both male and female robins stake out individual territories. The size of a territory varies a lot, and often depends on the amount of food available; a robin would only need a small area to itself, if this area had lots of bushes and plants, to provide it with food.

If you think that all robins look alike, look again. By taking close-up colour photographs in my own garden, I discovered that six different robins had been living there over a two year period.

In spring, the male robin is usually brighter than the female and he has a more noticeable greenish band at the edge of the

red breast. A female robin has a broader crown which gives her a square-headed look seen face-on. But each robin is an individual, especially in plumage. The brightness of the feathers varies according to age and season. Fledgling (young) robins resemble tiny thrushes (robins and thrushes belong to the same family) and do not get their coloured breast feathers until winter.

During winter months, when food is harder to find, the robin gets bolder, and it is during this time that you may be able to get one to take meal-worms and other treats from your hand. Later on, in spring, when more food is available, the robin will not be so easy to see, and its nest will probably be very difficult to find.

Nest-building usually starts in late March, depending on the weather. The nest foundation is nearly always of dry leaves (oak is their favourite) and grass topped by a cosy cup of moss and hair. Four or five off-white rusty speckled eggs are laid, one each morning, and incubated (sat on and warmed by the

parent bird) for 14 days. The nestlings are fed by both parents and fly at 14 days.

One of their favourite nest sites is a hole in a hedge bank. Other places are holes in trees, ivy-covered walls, tree trunks, and nest boxes. Robins' nests have been discovered in such strange places as in the mouth of a cod hung on a quayside; in a human skull; on a book shelf and under a car bonnet.

Push an old kettle or large boot into a bramble patch and there is every chance that a robin will take to it. An open garage window might also encourage robins (a pair made their home among the cans on a shelf in my own garage).

From start to finish, nest-building usually takes a couple of days, but the record must go to the pair which set up home in a gardener's jacket pocket. Between hanging up his coat at 9 a.m. and collecting it at 1 p.m. for lunch, a busy redbreast had made an almost complete nest. How's that for being Wide Awake?

A close-up of the robins' nest before the eggs hatched.

Ratty & Mole's Picnic

from The Wind in the Willows by Kenneth Grahame

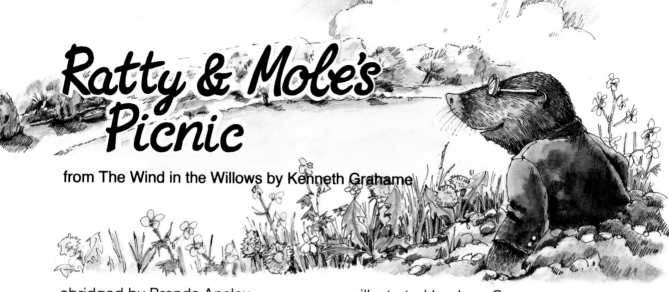

abridged by Brenda Apsley   illustrated by Jane Cope

The Mole had been working very hard all morning, spring cleaning his little home. First with brooms, then with dusters; then with a brush and white-wash, till he had dust in his throat and eyes, splashes of whitewash all over his black fur, and an aching back and weary arms. Spring was moving in the air above, and he suddenly flung his brush on the floor, said, "Bother!" and, "O blow!" and also, "Hang spring cleaning!" and bolted out of the house.

He scraped and scratched and scrabbled and scrooged, and then he scrooged again and scrabbled and scratched and scraped, working busily with his little paws and muttering to himself, "Up we go! Up we go!" till at last *pop!* his snout came out into the sunlight, and he found himself rolling in the warm grass of a meadow. "This is fine!" he said. "This is better than whitewashing!"

He meandered aimlessly along until he stood by the edge of a river. As he sat on the grass and looked across the river, a dark hole in the bank opposite caught his eye. Something bright and small seemed to twinkle down in the heart of it. Then the star winked at him and a small face appeared. A brown little face, with whiskers, small neat ears and thick silky hair. It was the Water Rat!

"Hello, Mole!" said the Water Rat. "Would you like to come over?"

The Rat stepped into a little boat painted blue outside and white within, and sculled smartly across the river. The Mole stepped down and found himself in a real boat. "I've never been in a boat before," he said.

"What?" cried the Rat. "Why, there is nothing half so much worth doing as messing about in boats – or with boats. In or out of 'em, it doesn't matter. Look here, suppose we go down the river together, and make a day of it?"

The Mole waggled his toes from sheer happiness. "Let's start at once!" he said.

"Hold hard a minute!" said the Rat. He climbed up into his hole and re-appeared staggering under a fat wicker picnic basket. "There's cold chicken inside," he said. "Coldtonguecoldham-coldbeefpickledgherkinssaladfrenchro-llscresssandwichespottedmeatgingerb-eerlemonadesodawater –"

"O, stop, stop," cried the Mole. "This is too much!"

"Do you think so?" asked the Rat. "It's only what I always take on these little excursions, and the other animals are always telling me that I'm a mean beast."

But the Mole didn't hear a word he was saying. He trailed a paw in the water and dreamed long, waking dreams while the Rat sculled steadily.

Presently the Rat brought the boat

alongside a bank, helped Mole ashore, and swung out the picnic basket. The Mole shook out the tablecloth, took out all the mysterious packets one by one, and arranged their contents, gasping, "O my! O my!" at each fresh relevation.

When all was ready the Rat said, "Now pitch in, old fellow!"

"Well," said the Rat presently, "I suppose we ought to be moving."

The afternoon sun was getting low as he sculled gently homewards. The Mole was already quite at home in a boat (so he thought) and he said, "Ratty, I want to row now."

The Rat shook his head with a smile. "Not yet," he said. "It's not as easy as it looks."

The Mole was quiet for a minute, then he jumped up and seized the sculls so suddenly that the Rat fell backwards off his seat with his legs in the air, while the Mole took his place and grabbed the sculls.

"Stop it!" cried the Rat. "You'll have us over!"

The Mole made a great dig at the water, missed, and his legs flew up above his head. He found himself lying on top of Rat. Greatly alarmed, he made a grab at the side of the boat, and the next moment – *sploosh!* – over went the

boat, and he found himself in the river. How cold the water was, and how very wet it felt. He went down, down, down, then a firm paw gripped him by the back of his neck. It was the Rat, who got a scull and shoved it under Mole's arm. Then he did the same at the other side and, swimming behind, propelled the helpless animal to the shore, hauled him out and sat him down, a squashy, pulpy lump of misery.

Mole, wet and ashamed, trotted about till he was fairly dry, while the Rat plunged into the water again, recovered the boat, fetched his floating property to shore, and finally dived successfully for the picnic basket and struggled to land with it.

When all was ready for a start once more, the Mole, limp and dejected, took his seat and said, "Ratty, I am very sorry for my foolish conduct. My heart quite fails me when I think how I might have lost that beautiful picnic basket. Will you forgive me?"

"That's all right," said the Rat. "What's a little wet to a Water Rat? I think you had better come and stop with me for a time. I'll teach you to row, and to swim."

The Mole was so touched that he could not answer, and he had to brush away a tear or two with the back of his paw.

When they got home the Rat made a bright fire and sat the Mole in an armchair in front of it, in dressing gown and slippers, and told him river stories till supper time. Stories about weirs, sudden floods, leaping pike, herons, and about adventures down drains, and night fishing with Otter.

Supper was a cheerful meal, but very shortly afterwards a terribly sleepy Mole had to be escorted to the best bedroom, where he soon laid his head on his pillow in great contentment, knowing that his new-found friend, the River, was lapping the sill of his window.

coldchickencoldtonguecoldhamcoldbeef-
pickledgherkinssaladfrenchrollscress-
sandwichespottedmeatgingerbeer-
lemonadesodawater . . .

If you want to enjoy a picnic like Ratty and Mole's, rule number one is KEEP IT SIMPLE. Don't choose food that takes hours to cook; take foods that are easy to pack and carry – and easy to eat!

If you can, take a rug to sit on, and a paper-cloth for the food. Use paper plates, and plastic knives and forks if you need them, though the food here can be eaten with just fingers and a spoon. Take wet wipes or paper napkins for wiping hands, plastic beakers for drinks (with curly crazy straws if you have them) and a carrier bag for rubbish.

And if the sun doesn't shine – have an indoor picnic!

Pitta Picnic Parcels

You can buy white or wholemeal pitta breads from delicatessens or supermarkets and they are perfect picnic food as they are easy to fill, carry – and eat. Allow one large pitta bread (halved) or two small pittas per person. Open them carefully to make 'pockets' and pack with some of these fillings:

Chicken and Apple Mayonnaise: Cut up some cooked chicken into small chunks, or use 2–3 slices of chicken roll, rolled into tubes. Dip thin apple chunks or slices in a little lemon juice, and shred some washed and dried lettuce. Spread the insides of the pittas with mayonnaise, and add the filling in layers, starting and finishing with lettuce.

Tongue and Orange: Roll up slices of cooked tongue (2 per pitta) and peel and skin some orange segments (or use tinned mandarin oranges, drained). Shred some lettuce and pack into the pitta parcels.

Beef and Coleslaw: Roll up slices of cooked beef, and shred some lettuce. Take a tub of coleslaw and, if you like horseradish (and Mole certainly did!) stir in a teaspoonful. Pile layers of lettuce, beef rolls and coleslaw into the pitta parcels.

Ham and Peaches: Roll up cooked ham slices, drain a tin of peach slices and cut into small chunks. If you like mayonnaise, spread it inside the pittas, then pack with layers of ham, peaches and shredded lettuce.

Potted Meat, Tomato and Cucumber: Spread the insides of the pittas thickly with potted meat, then add slices of cucumber and tomato, and a little shredded lettuce. If you don't like potted meat, try potted salmon instead, with the tomato and cucumber slices, and a few drops of lemon juice squeezed over.

If you don't eat meat, try these fillings:

Cheese and Peanut Butter: Spread the pittas with smooth peanut butter and add cheese slices or chunks. If you like them, add a couple of spring onions, and some shredded lettuce. A firm cheese like Cheddar or Edam is best.

Egg, Carrot and Green Pepper: Mash cooled hard-boiled eggs with a little mayonnaise and salt

and pepper to make egg mayonnaise, and spread inside the pittas. Cut the top off a green pepper, remove the seeds, and slice into thin rings. Peel and coarsely grate some carrot, and add the green pepper and grated carrot to the pitta.

* Instead of lettuce, you can use mustard and cress in your pitta parcels. Buy a box of cress, wash it under running cold water, and snip off with kitchen scissors. Cress tastes especially good with the egg filling.

* You can use the fillings in French rolls if you prefer. Split them lengthwise and take out some of the soft bread so that you can pack in lots of filling.

* If, like Ratty, you like pickled gherkins, add gherkin fans to your picnic parcels. Drain bottled gherkins, then make two or three cuts along their length, not quite to the end, and ease into fan shapes. Tuck into pittas or French rolls.

* Pack your pittas or rolls in tinfoil. This will keep them cool and fresh.

* Remember to take salt and pepper with you.

Superspecial Salads

Large coleslaw or cottage cheese tubs make good picnic salad carriers. Allow one carton per person and try these cottage cheese-based salad ideas:

Cottage Cheese, Peanuts and Raisins: Line a clean carton with lettuce leaves, then add cottage cheese, salted peanuts and raisins. Snap a lid on and you have an easy-to-carry, easy-to-eat individual picnic salad.

Cottage Cheese, Grapes and Apple: Line a carton with lettuce leaves, then fill with cottage cheese, seedless grapes and cubes of apple. Toss the apple in a little lemon juice to stop it discolouring.

Cottage Cheese, Celery and Orange: Line a carton as before, then add cottage cheese, finely chopped celery and peeled, skinned and chopped orange segments. You could try drained, tinned mandarin oranges, too.

Vegetable Dippers

For this dish, prepare some fresh salad vegetables:

Cos lettuce leaves, washed and dried

Radishes, washed, then topped and tailed

Carrots, peeled and cut into thin sticks

Button mushrooms, washed and dried

Cauliflower, washed and cut into small 'florets'

Tiny tomatoes, washed and dried

Pack the vegetables into a large foil parcel and pack some dips:

Hummus is a chick pea dip that you can buy in delicatessens and supermarkets. Carry it in a carton with a snap-on lid.

Minty Yogurt Dip is extra-easy – just stir a quarter teaspoon of dried mint into a small carton of plain yogurt. Pack in a lidded carton.

When you start your picnic, open out the foil parcel into a salad bowl shape, take the lids off the dips, and eat with fingers, dipping the vegetables.

Desserts

Picnic desserts should be very simple. Yogurts are good, and you can make them special by adding:

* diced apple pieces to muesli yogurt
* slices of banana to peach yogurt
* slices of fresh strawberry to strawberry yogurt
* grated dark chocolate to orange yogurt

Pack yogurt desserts into clean, small, lidded cartons – and remember spoons!

If you want to go to a bit more trouble, make:

Fruity Kebabs

Prepare cubes of peeled fruit – apple, orange, banana, pear – plus some whole strawberries, tinned pineapple chunks and glacé cherries. Toss the fruit in a

little lemon juice, or a mixture of orange and lemon juice, and thread onto wooden kebab sticks. Wrap in foil, one kebab per person. These look very colourful, and taste good, too.

Thirst Quenchers

Ratty's Old Fashioned Lemonade

3 lemons
175g/6oz sugar
900ml/1½ pints boiling water

1. Wash the lemons, dry, and peel off the rind thinly with a potato peeler.
2. Put the lemon rind and sugar into a large mixing basin and pour on the boiling water. **IMPORTANT: Boiling water is dangerous. You must get a parent or adult to help with this.**
3. Cover and cool in the 'fridge, stirring from time to time.
4. Squeeze the juice from the lemons and add to the basin.
5. Strain the lemonade through a sieve.

Chill the lemonade and take to the picnic in a large, wide-necked flask. Makes just over 1 litre/ 2 pints.

Ginger Beer is not easy to make, and takes a few days, so for a picnic, buy a bottle of ginger beer, chill it well, and carry in a wide-necked flask.

Orange Soda is quick and easy. Just mix equal amounts of fresh, pure orange juice and soda water, chill, and carry in a flask.

by Brenda Apsley

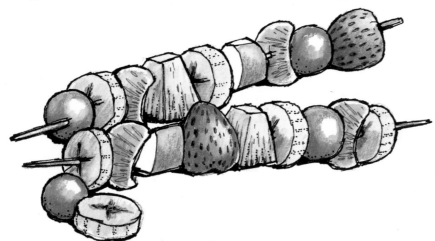

Knit a Brownie Doll

by Dorothy Bramble

photograph by Hope Palmer

Materials required

Small amounts of double knitting wool in tan, brown, fawn and pink. A pair of size 11 (3¾ mm) needles. Stuffing. Small pieces of black and red felt for eyes and nose and a small amount of red wool to embroider mouth.

ABBREVIATIONS

st stitch   s.s. stocking stitch (one row knit and one row purl)   dec. decrease   inc increase   K. knit   P. purl   tog together   rep repeat   beg beginning

SKIRT

With tan wool cast on 50 sts and K. 3 rows. Then beginning with a knit row s.s. 12 rows. Dec row (K.3 K.2 tog) to the end (40 sts) P. one row.
Leave these sts on a spare needle.

POCKETS (make two)

Cast on 6 sts and s.s. 6 rows. Cast off.

BODY

With tan wool cast on 40 sts s.s. 10 rows
Next row K. the 1st st from the skirt with the 1st st from the body tog then K. 2nd st from the skirt with the 2nd st from the body tog and continue across the row. With dark brown wool s.s. 4 rows (for belt) change back to tan wool and beginning with a P. row, s.s. 15 rows.
Dec row K.6 K.2 tog K.4 K.2 tog K.12 K.2 tog K.4 K.2 tog K.6   Purl one row
Dec row K.5 K.2 tog K.4 K.2 tog K.10 K.2 tog K.4 K.2 tog K.5   Purl one row
Dec row K.4 K.2 tog K.4 K.2 tog K.8 K.2 tog K.4 K.2 tog K.4   Cast off.

HEAD

With pink wool cast on 28 sts and s.s. 2 rows
Inc row K.4 inc in next st K.4 inc in next st K.8 inc in next st K.4 inc in next st K.4   Purl one row
Inc row K.5 inc in next st K.4 inc in next st K.10 inc in next st K.4 inc in next st K.5   Purl one row
Inc row K.6 inc in next st K.4 inc in next st K.12 inc in next st K.4 inc in next st K.6
Beg with a purl row s.s. 21 rows
Next row K.2 tog all across then cast off tightly.

LEGS (make two)

With fawn wool cast on 18 st and s.s. 11 rows then K.1 row P.1 row. Change to pink wool and beg with a P. row s.s. 13 rows. Cast off.

ARMS (make two)

Cast on 16 sts with tan wool and s.s. 16 rows. Change to pink wool and s.s. 8 rows.
Dec. row K.2 tog all across. Cast off tightly.

FEET (make two)

With brown wool cast on 10 sts and s.s. 6 rows
Next row inc in 1st st K.8 inc in last st (12 sts) s.s. 4 rows
Next row K.2 tog K.8 K.2 tog (10 sts) P. 1 row

Next row K.2 tog K.6 K.2 tog (8 sts) P. 1 row
Next row Inc in first st K.6 inc in last st (10 sts) P. 1 row
Next row inc in first st K.8 inc in last st (12 sts) s.s. 4 rows
Next row K.2 tog K.8 K.2 tog (10 sts) s.s. 5 rows
Next row K.2 tog K.6 K.2 tog (8 sts) Cast off.

HAT

With brown wool cast on 50 st.
1st row K.2 * (P.1 K.1) to end of row
Repeat this row 21 times
Next row K.2 * (P.1 K.1) 3 times K.2 tog repeat from * to end
Next row * P.2 (K.1 P.1) twice K.1 rep from * to end
Next row K.2 * (P.1 K.1) twice P.1 K.2 tog rep from * to end
Next row P.1 K.1 to end of row
Next row K.2 * (P.1 K.1) twice K.2 tog rep from * to end
Next row P.2 * K.1 P.1 K.1 repeat from * to end
Next row K.2 * P.1 K.1 P.1 K.2 tog rep from * to end
Next row P.1 K.1 to end
Next row K.2 * P.1 K.1 K.2 tog rep from * to end
Next row * P.2 K.1 rep from * to end
Next row K.2 * P.1 K.2 tog rep from * to end
Next row P.2 tog all across
Cast off tightly.

COLLAR

With tan wool cast on 34 sts and K.1 row
Next row K.2 tog K.30 K.2 tog.   P.1 row
Next row K.2 tog K.28 K.2 tog.   P.1 row
Cast off.

TO MAKE UP

Sew seam in body and skirt. Place seam at centre back and sew across bottom of the body. Stuff and sew up neck.
Sew back seam of head and draw top (cast off edge) as close as possible. Stuff and sew neck edge. Sew neck edge of body to neck edge of head.
Sew collar round neck making front edges meet.
Sew seams of legs and across the bottom (fawn for socks). Stuff. Sew tops of legs and then sew legs side by side to lower edge of body. Sew sides of feet. Stuff and sew to bottom of legs.
Make a tie from yellow felt as diagram and pin under collar with a miniature Brownie badge.
Embroider Brownie emblem on left breast and make eyes from black felt and nose from red felt and embroider a mouth on face.
Sew seam of hat and turn back about ¾" for brim. Sew strands of yellow wool onto head for hair and tie into two bunches at sides of head. Sew hat to head and make a small woollen bobble to go on hat.

A LEGOLAND village scene — you can see some real people in the background.

The temple of Abu Simbel.

The Amalienborg in Copenhagen, the Danish royal family's home. It took 900,000 LEGO bricks to build it.

The LEGO Story

A Modern Fairytale

by Brenda Apsley

Once upon a time, a poor joiner and carpenter called Ole Kirk Christiansen started a business in a tiny workshop in Billund, Denmark. He made ladders and milking stools for the local farmers, and toys for their children, until the early 1930s, when work became scarce. Ole had to do something to keep his business going . . .

What he did was to think up some new products — especially wooden children's toys, which sold well, and became the firm's future. He called his toys LEGO from the Danish words *LEg GOdt*, which mean play well.

The business grew, and Ole's son Godtfred joined his father. In the 1950s he made a trip to England, and on the boat met a buyer from a big Copenhagen store. "What the toy market needs is a product with a system," the buyer told Godtfred. "A toy for boys and girls, suitable for all year use, and one that will develop a child's imagination and creativity."

The result was the LEGO brick building system. It sounds simple — blocks of coloured plastic with

A docks scene, with bridges, cranes — and moving ships.

At LEGOLAND, even the giraffes are made of LEGO bricks!

Though LEGO bricks are a simple shape and design, they can be fitted together in endless combinations:

Two 8-stud bricks of the same colour can be fitted together in 24 different ways.

Three 8-stud bricks of the same colour can be fitted together in 1,060 ways.

With six 8-stud bricks the possible number of combinations zooms up to more than 100 million (102,981,500 to be exact!).

The LEGO model of the Mount Rushmore mountain carving took sculptor Bjorn Richter nine months to complete.

studs and tubes that fit together — but as anyone who has played with LEGO soon realises, the possibilities are endless.

The LEGO system became popular almost immediately, and is now exported to more than one hundred countries. Millions of people, young and old, love playing with LEGO, for it can be built into — well, just about anything — as the pictures here show.

Most people could make a LEGO house or boat, but LEGOLAND shows what the experts can do with time, talent — and millions of bricks!

LEGOLAND was opened by Godtfred in 1968 beside the original factory at Billund to show the amazing possibilities of LEGO bricks.

There are towns and villages, the Copenhagen docks with moving trains and ships, the Danish royal palace, the Acropolis, and the temple of Rameses II — all perfect scale models made with nothing but LEGO bricks. There are also LEGO men, women and children, LEGO pigs, sheep, cows and wild animals, and LEGO helicopters,

jets, trains and ships. Perhaps the most ambitious model is a scaled-down reproduction of America's Mount Rushmore carving which features the faces of four presidents — Roosevelt, Jefferson, Washington and Lincoln — hacked out of a mountainside. The LEGOLAND version stands about 13.5 metres high, and sculptor Bjorn Richter used 1,500,000 bricks to build it, plus about 40,000 larger-sized junior bricks.

There are more than 30 million bricks in all in LEGOLAND . . . and to think that the LEGO story started when a poor carpenter devised a simple children's building brick!

LEGO is popular all over the world, and regularly appears in lists of top-selling toys. It has been estimated that some 50,000,000 children spend about 4,000,000,000 hours every year playing with LEGO!

can and you will, or I'll have you beheaded!"

There was a scuffle in the crowd and the helicopter mechanic darted forward and bent low at the king's feet.

"Majesty," he murmured reverently, "Majesty. I am the prince's helicopter pilot, mechanic and aide. Prince Florizel is overcome with shock and gratitude. Is that not so, Sire?" he asked, turning to the prince.

"Um, yes, yes, that's right," said the prince nervously.

"Prince Florizel, of course, must have the blessing of *his* father, the King of Buzzaramia, whose kingdom adjoins your own, before the ceremony can take place. Is that not so, Sire?"

"Definitely," said the prince.

"Quite, quite," said the king, "I favour these old customs myself.

The princess will fly there tomorrow to meet him, in her own royal helicopter."

"And I shall pilot myself," said the princess.

"We shan't go into *that* now," said the king. "Here, you may kiss the princess."

With a small sigh, the prince fainted dead away.

"Shock," said the pilot hastily. "Clearly shock, Your Majesty. It's not every day he wins the hand of such a beautiful, charming and talented young lady." And he looked into the princess's eyes.

The prince was carried out to his helicopter and flown off by his pilot, with instructions that Princess Ermyntrude would fly to Buzzaramia the following day.

Next morning she was up early and, dressed in her frog-green

flying suit and bright red aviator goggles, she slipped out to her helicopter before the king was up. She climbed in and was just warming up the engine when the Lord Chamberlain came rushing out into the garden. "Your Highness, the king says you cannot go without him," he spluttered.

Princess Ermyntrude turned off the master switch and leaned out of the window.

"Well, he'd better hurry and I'm piloting," she said carelessly. "I'll wait three minutes and I'm going if he hasn't come by then."

The Lord Chamberlain rushed into the palace and returned with the king, who was hastily pulling his ermine robe over his nightshirt and replacing his night-cap with a crown.

"You're a dreadful girl, Ermyntrude," he said sadly.

"I'm *not*," said Ermyntrude. "Anyway, all this was your idea. I'm not marrying that silly prince and I'm flying over to tell him so."

"Ermyntrude," cried the king, scandalized. "How can you do such a thing? I'll be ruined. He won the contest. And besides, you've got to marry someone."

"I haven't and I won't," said the princess firmly and she set the rotor blades in action.

Within an hour, they were flying into the next kingdom and soon they could see the palace shining golden on the highest hilltop.

"Over there," said the king mournfully. "Please change your mind, Ermyntrude."

"Never!" said the princess positively. "Never, never, never, never, never!"

Below them they could see the landing pad with ostrich feathers and fairy-lights along the strip. Princess Ermyntrude settled the helicopter gently on the ground, waited for the blades to stop turning and got out. The prince's mechanic was standing on the tarmac.

"A perfect landing," he cried admiringly.

Princess Ermyntrude smiled. Just then, an older man in ermine trimmed pyjamas came running across the grass.

continued from page 9

"Florizel, Florizel, what is all this?" he cried.

The mechanic picked up an oilcan from beside his feet.

"Put that down you ninny," cried the man in ermine pyjamas. "Don't you know this is a royal princess?"

"You're being ridiculous, Father," said the mechanic. "Of course I know she's a princess. I'm going to marry her."

"*You* are?" cried the Princess Ermyntrude's father. "My daughter's not marrying you. She's marrying your prince."

"I am marrying him," said Princess Ermyntrude.

"She certainly is," said the mechanic. "And in case you're wondering, I *am* Prince Florizel. The other one was an impostor."

"But how?" asked the princess.

"Well," said Prince Florizel, "it was my father's idea that I should go, so I persuaded my mechanic to change places with me. I thought my father would never find out. Then, when I saw Princess Ermyntrude, I fell in love with her instantly. She had axle grease on her neck and she was so big and strong. Then I realized it was lucky I'd changed places, or you'd have eliminated me on height."

"That's right. You're too short," said the king.

"He's not," said the princess.

"No, I'm not, I'm exactly right and so is she," said Prince Florizel. "When I saw her pulling faces and shouting insults and throwing princes to the ground, I knew she was the one person I could fall in love with."

"Really?" asked the princess.

"Truly," said Prince Florizel. "Now, come and see my mechanical digger."

And holding the oilcan in one hand and the princess's hand in the other, he led the way to the machine shed.

The king looked at Prince Florizel's father. "There's nothing I can do with her once she's made up her mind," he said wearily.

"I have the same trouble with Florizel," said the second king.

"I say, would you like some breakfast?"

"Would I?" said the princess's father, "I certainly would."

So arm-in-arm they went off together to the palace.

And so Princess Ermyntrude and Prince Florizel were married in tremendous splendour. Princess Ermyntrude had a special diamond and gold thread boiler suit made for the wedding and she drove herself to the church in a beautiful bright red fork-lift truck with E in flashing lights on one side and F picked out in stars on the other and with garlands of flowers on the forks.

Prince Florizel, who had parachuted in for the wedding, wore an emerald and silver thread shirt with silver lamé trousers and had flowers in his beard. On the steps of the church he reached up on tiptoe to kiss the princess as the television cameras whirred and the people cheered, then they ran down the steps and jumped into the royal fork-lift and steered away through the excited crowds.

"I'm so terribly happy," murmured the prince.

"So am I," said the princess. "I say, did you bring the hamburgers and the ketchup?"

"All there in the back," said the prince.

"And I remembered the wedding cake. Look at it," said the princess proudly.

"Good heavens," cried Prince Florizel. "It's magnificent." For the wedding cake was shaped like a giant oilcan.

"Perfect, don't you think?" murmured the princess.

"Absolutely," said the prince.

And they both lived happily ever after.

The Wrestling Princess and other stories **by Judy Corbalis**
were first published in 1986 by Andre Deutsch Limited, and the title story is reproduced here by kind permission.

Illustrations © 1986 by Helen Craig

HOW DOES YOUR GARDEN GROW?

by Brenda Apsley

Quickly and prettily, if you 'grow' a paper collage garden like this one. Here's how to make one for yourself:

Work on a rectangular piece of thick paper or card; the front of a cereal box is ideal. You also need a pencil, some quick-

First, decide on the 'look' of your paper garden. Will it have lots of conifers and greenery and just a few striking plants? Will it have stretches of smooth green lawn and neat rose beds? Will there be stone walls, steps, a pond or a fountain? Or will it be a

Next, start to collect the paper cut-outs that will appear in your 'garden'. Cut out walls, fences, lawns etc, and as many trees, bushes, shrubs and plants as you can. Patches of blue sky are also useful. Cut around the plants as carefully as you can

drying glue, scissors – and lots of trees, bushes and flowers to 'plant' in your paper garden. Seed and plant catalogues are ideal for these. Ask parents or friends for out of date catalogues, or send off for some – they are often advertised in Sunday newspapers, and cost no more than a stamp.

busy cottage garden like the one shown here, with a riot of colourful flowers and bushes? When you have your idea, draw a very rough outline of where the main features will be.

using a small pair of scissors. Rounded outlines are easier to cut out than feathery ones, so try to find trees and flowers with bold, clear silhouettes. The more carefully you cut out the shapes, the better the finished collage will be.

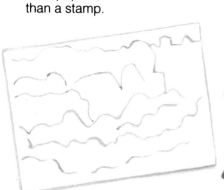

Before you stick anything down, move the paper shapes around on the card to try out different combinations of shape and colour. Try soft pinks against blue-green conifers, an all-white garden with coppery trees in the background, a colourful rose garden, a spring garden crammed with yellow daffodils and red tulips, or a multi-coloured cottage garden like the one shown here.

When your paper garden is finished, hang it in your room, or give one as a gift. A smaller version on white card folded down the middle would make a lovely, personal greetings card, or you could use this method to plan a real area of garden, trying out different plants and flowers on paper before planting.

illustrated by Linda Sandey

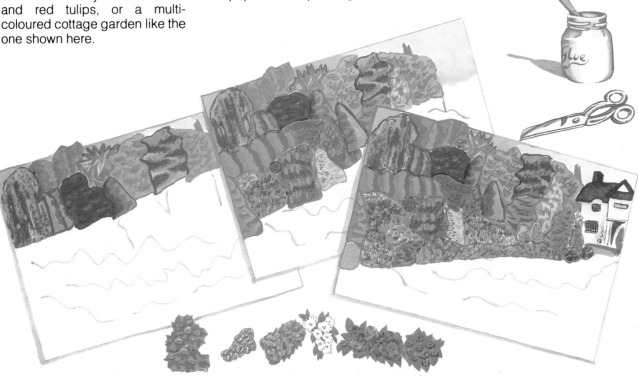

When you are ready to start sticking your paper shapes onto the card, start from a main focal point. Here we started with the house and let the garden grow around and in front of it. Position tall trees and hedges to form the background of the garden, leaving some blue sky showing, then work towards the foreground adding taller bushes, then smaller plants and finally edging and border plants. Overlap the paper plants carefully so that all the background card is covered to give a natural, busy look. Glue down the paper edges carefully, smoothing down each shape and wiping away excess glue as you work.

Get on the right tracks and take a day trip around the world in our

GREAT RAIL RIDERS COMPETITION

Trains are really going places these days – and they're getting there faster than ever.

British Rail operates the fastest diesel trains in the world, and most InterCity trains burn up the tracks at over 100 mph for mile after mile on every journey.

Model trains, too, are just as exciting as the real thing, and first prize in this year's competition sponsored by British Rail is the chance to see both big and small trains in action during a day when you'll go "round the world"

The world you'll see is Rail Riders World, probably the largest model railway layout in the country. It's actually on York railway station and has over 400 metres of 00 gauge track with up to 14 different trains running at any one time: 2,500 tiny people, 600 buildings and more than 5,500 trees and shrubs are packed into realistic backgrounds. The whole modern British Rail scene is on display with high speed trains, modern diesels and electrics, freight trains and even the Orient Express and the Royal Train.

Answers to puzzles on page 17

Brownie Crossword

Riddle-me-Ree
Answer: Brownies are fun.

Puzzle Square 'A'

	¹P	U	R	L	²
	A			O	
	C	A		S	
	³K	I	T	E	

Alice · Rita
Pat · Prue
Ailsa · Katie
Laura · Celia
Lois · Clara
Sue · Core
Paula · Clare
Louise · Cleo
Sara · Claire
Elsa

Puzzle Square 'B'

	¹S	T	E	W	
	A		E		
	C	B	S		
	³K	I	L	T	

Sew · Ski · Sable
Steal · Skate · Swat
Stalk · Stab · Salt
Slack · Sect · Silk
Seat · Skit · Sweat
Sleet · Sail · Steak
Slit · Seal · Silt
Stilt · Stable · Sweet
Slab · Slate · Seek
Set · Slat · Sleek